Inspire English International

Year 8 Workbook

Ben Hulme-Cross

Contents

About the Workbook — iv

Unit 1: Heroes and villains
1 Telling stories — 6
2 Building a character — 10
3 Creating danger — 14
4 Openings — 18
5 Assessment — 22
6 Story structure — 24
7 Endings — 28
8 Ways of telling stories — 32
9 Structuring sentences — 36
10 Reviewing, revising and proofreading — 40
11 Assessment — 44

Unit 2: Safe and sound
1 Spotting persuasive techniques — 46
2 Persuasive vocabulary — 50
3 Responding to a text — 54
4 Organising your response — 58
5 Assessment — 62
6 Persuasive paragraphs — 64
7 Persuasive structures — 68
8 Exploring the writer's choices — 72
9 Rhetorical devices — 76
10 Getting ready to respond — 80
11 Assessment — 84

Unit 3: A perfect world
1 Exploring a fictional future — 86
2 Building an argument — 90
3 Choosing vocabulary 1 — 94
4 Choosing vocabulary 2 — 98
5 Assessment — 102
6 Supporting key points — 104
7 Structuring sentences — 108
8 Using rhetorical devices — 112
9 Introductions and conclusions — 116
10 Reviewing and revising — 120
11 Assessment — 124

Contents

Unit 4: World of sport

1	Summarising	126
2	Informing and describing	130
3	Selecting evidence	134
4	Exploring vocabulary choice	138
5	Writing a response	142
6	Assessment	146
7	Structuring an information text	148
8	Exploring vocabulary and sentence choices	152
9	Planning a critical response	156
10	Comparing information texts	160
11	Assessment	164

Unit 5: A moment in time

1	Writing autobiographically	166
2	Exploring structure and intention	170
3	Using narrative structure	174
4	Choosing precise vocabulary	178
5	Assessment	182
6	Expressing feelings	184
7	Structuring paragraphs	188
8	Experimenting with sentences	192
9	Experimenting with openings	196
10	Experimenting with endings	200
11	Assessment	204

Unit 6: Dramatic!

1	Curtain up	206
2	Setting the scene	210
3	From page to stage	214
4	Creating conflict	218
5	Crafting characters	222
6	Assessment	226
7	Shakespearean speech	228
8	Performing	232
9	Exploring themes	236
10	Introductions and conclusions	240
11	Assessment	244

About the Workbook

Welcome to Inspire English International! We hope you will find this book useful (and inspiring!) as you develop your skill and knowledge in written English. Through explicitly addressing the areas needed to excel in English you should gain mastery of the subject and make excellent progress.

The books have been written using a mix of real-world texts and purpose-written passages, designed to inspire discussion and help to maintain a focus on key curriculum objectives.

This Workbook gives you the chance to practise and embed the key skills introduced in the Student Book and through teaching, thereby deepening and broadening your understanding. Clear links are provided between this book and the Student Book and daily teaching, to support this further.

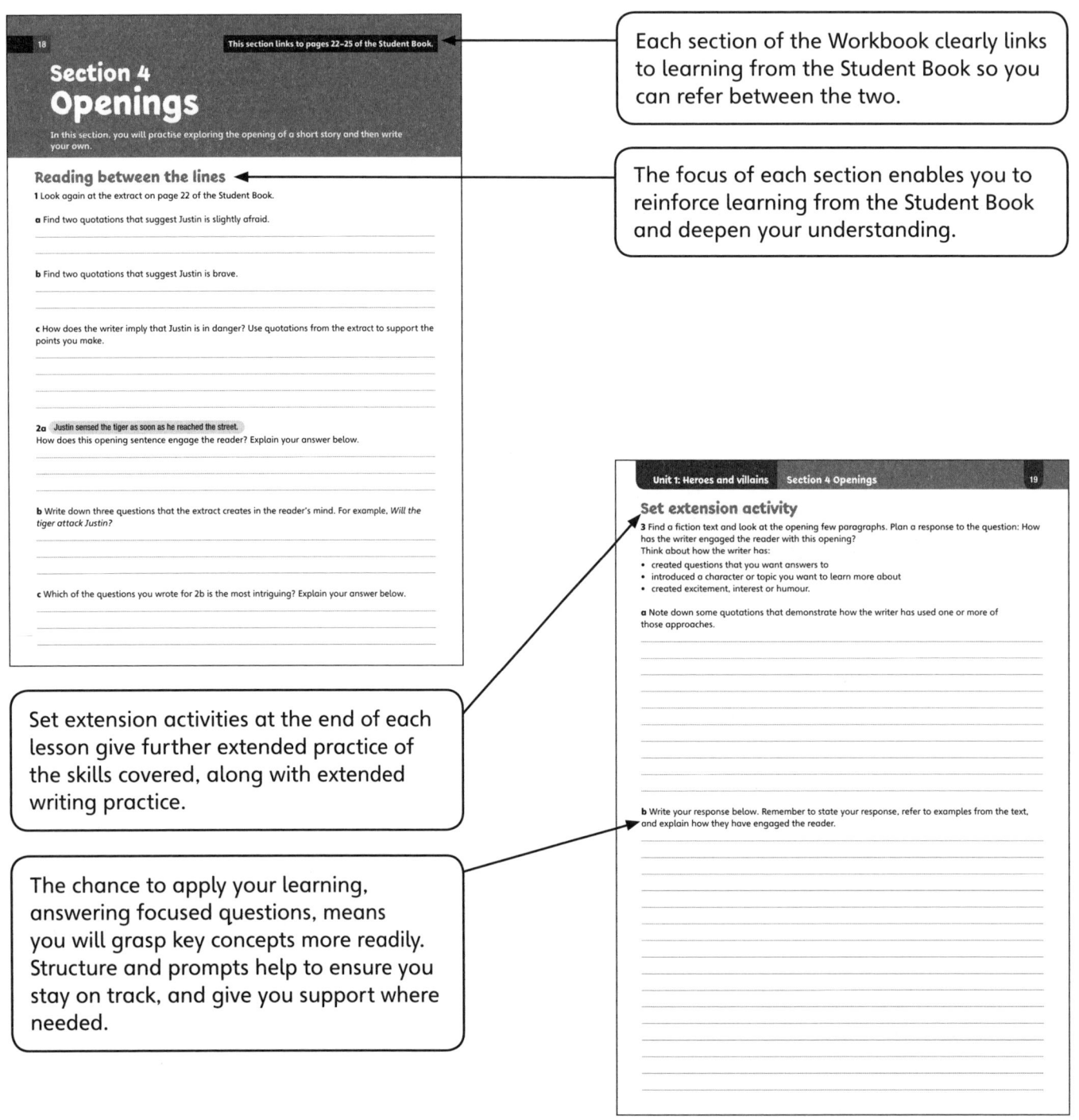

Each section of the Workbook clearly links to learning from the Student Book so you can refer between the two.

The focus of each section enables you to reinforce learning from the Student Book and deepen your understanding.

Set extension activities at the end of each lesson give further extended practice of the skills covered, along with extended writing practice.

The chance to apply your learning, answering focused questions, means you will grasp key concepts more readily. Structure and prompts help to ensure you stay on track, and give you support where needed.

About the Workbook

Innovative assessment sections explain clearly how to proofread and improve a response, and then give you the chance to put your learning into practice.

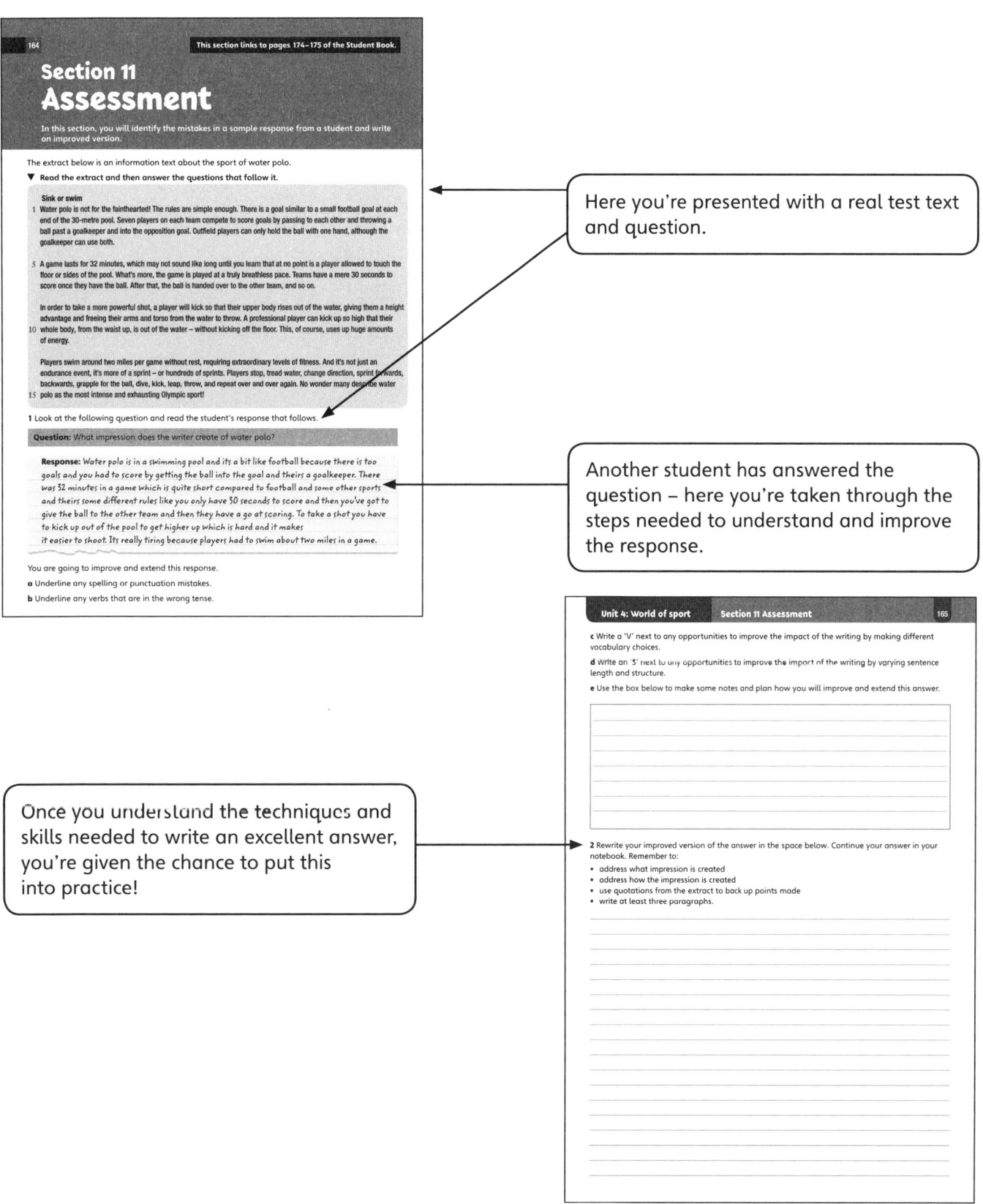

Here you're presented with a real test text and question.

Another student has answered the question – here you're taken through the steps needed to understand and improve the response.

Once you understand the techniques and skills needed to write an excellent answer, you're given the chance to put this into practice!

This section links to pages 10–13 of the Student Book.

Section 1
Telling stories

In this section, you will practise exploring different ways to tell stories and make them successful.

Identifying key points

1 Look again at Extract A on page 10 of the Student Book and answer the following questions.

a Why does Eurystheus keep setting Heracles tasks?

_____

_____

b How has Heracles responded to the tasks so far?

_____

_____

c What is the new task that Eurystheus sets Heracles?

_____

_____

Active and passive voices

2 Rewrite the sentences below in the active voice.

a The dog was tricked by the man.

_____

b The king was infuriated by the man's success.

_____

c The goddess was not surprised by the king's failure.

_____

Characters

3 Using a quotation from Extract A, answer the following question: What are the goddess Hera's feelings about Heracles?

_____

_____

_____

Unit 1: Heroes and villains | **Section 1 Telling stories**

Set extension activity

4a Rewrite Extract B from page 12 of the Student Book in the first person, so that the story is told in the active voice by Heracles himself. Continue your answer in your notebook if needed.

b Now rewrite Extract B in the first person, so that the story is told in the active voice by the king himself. Continue your answer in your notebook if needed.

c Which version do you think is most likely to make the reader want to know more? Explain your answer below.

Comparing two texts

5 Look again at the two extracts on pages 10 and 12 of the Student Book.

a Which of the following statements do you most agree with?
 (i) *A good opening to a story makes the reader eager to read on.*
 (ii) *A good opening to a story gives the reader the background information they need to know.*
Explain your answer below.

_____
_____
_____
_____

b Which extract provides more information? Why do you think the writer has chosen to give more information in this extract?

_____
_____
_____
_____

c Which extract creates the strongest sense of mood or atmosphere? How has the writer achieved this effect? Support your response with quotations from the extract.

_____
_____
_____
_____

d Note down the key similarities and differences between the two extracts in the table below.

Key differences	Key similarities

e Which extract has the most exciting opening? How has the writer made it more exciting?

_____
_____
_____
_____

Unit 1: Heroes and villains — Section 1 Telling stories

Set extension activity

6a In Extract B, on page 12 of the Student Book, Heracles is presented as nervous. Rewrite this meeting with Cerberus, presenting Heracles as a fearless hero. Continue your answer in your notebook if needed.

b Look back over what you have written in **Activity 6a** above and reread Extract B. Make some notes below on key similarities and differences between Extract B and your version.

Key differences	Key similarities

c Which version – Extract B or your own version – do you feel is the most effective way of opening the story? Explain your answer below.

Section 2
Building a character

This section links to pages 14–17 of the Student Book.

In this section, you will practise exploring how a writer creates a villainous character, and then create your own villain.

Inferring character

1a Use the space below to note down all the quotations you can find in the extract on page 14 of the Student Book that show something about Walter Hartright's character.

_____
_____
_____

b Complete the following sentences. Use your own words and at least one quotation from the extract.

(i) The writer presents Walter as brave when _____
_____
_____
_____

(ii) Walter knows that he is in danger because _____
_____
_____
_____

2a Write a line of dialogue, spoken by Walter, to follow on from the end of the extract. Use it to show something about his character.
_____
_____

b Write an alternative to dialogue to follow on from the end of the extract. This time, instead of speaking, Walter does something. Use it to show something about his character.
_____
_____

c Choose your favourite option for extending the story from your answers to 2a and 2b above. How does what you have written show something about Walter's character?
_____
_____
_____

Unit 1: Heroes and villains — Section 2 Building a character

Set extension activity

3a Think of three villains from stories or films you know who made a big impression on you. Make some notes about them in the tables below.

Name	
Physical description	
Nastiest things about them	

Name	
Physical description	
Nastiest things about them	

Name	
Physical description	
Nastiest things about them	

b What do you think makes the best villains so memorable? Explain your answer below.

Revealing a villain

4a Select three quotations from the extract on page 14 of the Student Book that suggest Count Fosco is a villain.

_____
_____
_____
_____

b Which one shows us most clearly that he is a villain? Explain your answer below.

_____
_____
_____
_____

Planning a villain

5 You are going to plan your own villainous character. Imagine that they have moved in next door to where you live. Use the prompts below to plan a scene that introduces your villain to readers.

a What does the villain look like?

_____
_____
_____
_____

b What makes you first suspect they are a villain?

_____
_____
_____
_____

c How does what they do in the scene show that they are a villain?

_____
_____
_____
_____
_____

d How does what they say in the scene show that they are a villain?

_____
_____
_____
_____

Unit 1: Heroes and villains — Section 2 Building a character

Set extension activity

6a Write a scene that introduces your villainous character for the first time. Remember to focus on showing that they are a villain through their words, actions and reactions.

b Look back over what you have written and write a response to the following question: How has the writer (you) shown that this character is a villain?

Section 3
Creating danger

This section links to pages 18–21 of the Student Book.

In this section, you will practise exploring ways of creating tense, exciting action in a story.

Tracking danger

1 Look again at the extract on page 18 of the Student Book. For each paragraph:
- write a one-sentence summary of the danger Alex faces.
- select the quotation from that paragraph that most powerfully creates the sense of danger.

An example is provided.

Paragraph 1: Alex is nearly discovered by two men.
Quotation: 'Alex threw himself into the only hiding place available'

Paragraph 2: _____
Quotation: _____

Paragraph 3: _____
Quotation: _____

Paragraph 4: _____
Quotation: _____

Paragraph 5: _____
Quotation: _____

Paragraph 6: _____
Quotation: _____

2 Write a short response, using quotations from the extract as evidence, to the following question: How does the writer use Alex's physical sensations to create a sense of danger?

_____
_____
_____
_____
_____

Unit 1: Heroes and villains | **Section 3 Creating danger** | 15

Set extension activity

3 The writer of the extract on page 18 of the Student Book has focused on action by describing events in detail. You are going to rewrite the extract, focusing more on Alex's emotions and physical sensations.

a Make some notes on the emotions or physical sensations you could add into each paragraph of the extract.

_____
_____
_____
_____
_____
_____
_____

b Now write your new version of the extract. Continue your answer in your notebook if needed.

_____
_____
_____
_____
_____
_____
_____
_____
_____
_____
_____
_____
_____
_____

c Look back over what you have written and reread the extract on page 18 of the Student Book. Which version do you think is more effective? Explain your answer below.

_____
_____
_____
_____

Set extension activity
_____

Vocabulary choices

4a Look again at paragraph 4 of the extract on page 18 of the Student Book. Note down two verbs the writer uses that help to create a sense of physical force or violence.

_____

b Write one or two sentences explaining how the writer's choice of verbs in this paragraph helps to create a sense of violence.

_____

_____

_____

5 Look again at paragraph 5 of the extract.

a Note down two powerful adjectives that the writer uses to create a sense of danger.

_____

b Write one or two sentences explaining how the writer's choice of adjectives in this paragraph helps to create a sense of danger.

_____

_____

_____

Creating danger

6 You are going to begin to plan a scene in a story in which the main character faces danger. The character has fallen into a fast-flowing river and almost drowns. She manages to get to the safety of the shore, only to discover that a greater danger awaits her there. Make some notes using the prompts below to outline the action in the scene.

a How does she feel as the water sweeps her along?

_____

b How does she get to the shore?

_____

c How does she feel when she gets to the shore?

_____

d What is the new danger that awaits her there?

_____

e How does she react to the new danger?

_____

| Unit 1: Heroes and villains | Section 3 Creating danger |

Set extension activity

7 Continue to plan the scene from your story that you started planning in **Activity 6**.

a Note down any particularly strong verbs, nouns, adverbs or adjectives that you might use to create a sense of the danger the character is in, and the fear they experience.

Danger	Fear

b Write two or three paragraphs from your scene in the space provided. Remember to use powerful vocabulary to create a sense of danger. Remember that you can create a sense of danger by:

- telling the reader what is happening
- telling the reader what will happen soon
- focusing on physical sensations
- focusing on emotions.

Section 4
Openings

This section links to pages 22–25 of the Student Book.

In this section, you will practise exploring the opening of a short story and then write your own.

Reading between the lines

1 Look again at the extract on page 22 of the Student Book.

a Find two quotations that suggest Justin is slightly afraid.

_____
_____

b Find two quotations that suggest Justin is brave.

_____
_____

c How does the writer imply that Justin is in danger? Use quotations from the extract to support the points you make.

_____
_____
_____
_____

2a `Justin sensed the tiger as soon as he reached the street.`
How does this opening sentence engage the reader? Explain your answer below.

_____
_____
_____

b Write down three questions that the extract creates in the reader's mind. For example, *Will the tiger attack Justin?*

_____
_____
_____

c Which of the questions you wrote for 2b is the most intriguing? Explain your answer below.

_____
_____
_____

Unit 1: Heroes and villains — **Section 4 Openings**

Set extension activity

3 Find a fiction text and look at the opening few paragraphs. Plan a response to the question: How has the writer engaged the reader with this opening?
Think about how the writer has:

- created questions that you want answers to
- introduced a character or topic you want to learn more about
- created excitement, interest or humour.

a Note down some quotations that demonstrate how the writer has used one or more of those approaches.

b Write your response below. Remember to state your response, refer to examples from the text, and explain how they have engaged the reader.

Choosing tense and person

4 Read the following extract and then answer the questions.

He could hear the wolves' feet behind him now. It wouldn't be long. He ran on blindly, and then a low snarl sent shockwaves down his spine. He stumbled and fell to the ground, wet leaves filling his mouth.

a Rewrite the short extract above in the first person, present tense. For example, *I can hear.*

_____
_____
_____

b Look back over the original extract and your own version. Which is more engaging? Explain your answer below.

_____
_____
_____

Writing an opening

5 You are going to write an opening to your own story. The setting is a residential school trip. You are camping with your friends. You wake up and realise you have been sleep-walking. You can just make out the tents in the moonlight, some distance away. As you begin to walk towards them, something makes you aware that you are in danger. Make some notes using the prompts below to outline your opening.

a What is the immediate setting? For example, road, forest, beach. What vocabulary could you use to describe the setting and create a frightening atmosphere?

_____
_____
_____

b What warns you of the danger and what is the danger?

_____
_____
_____

c What happens next, once you sense the danger?

_____
_____

6 Write the opening to your story in your notebook. Aim to write three paragraphs. Remember to include some description of your feelings as you face the danger and to use the correct tense and person throughout.

Unit 1: Heroes and villains — **Section 4 Openings**

Set extension activity

7 Revise the skills you have covered in the first half of this unit, ready for the assessment in the next lesson. You may find it helpful to note down the key points covered in each of the sections so far. If there are any areas where you do not feel confident, reread the appropriate pages in the Student Book.

Section 1: Telling stories

When answering questions on a text, check that you have included all the relevant information.

Section 2: Building a character

Section 3: Creating danger

Section 4: Openings

Section 5
Assessment

In this section, you will answer questions on a short extract and improve a sample response from a student.

The extract below is taken from the short story *The Tell-Tale Heart* by Edgar Allen Poe.

▼ **Read the extract and then answer the questions that follow it.**

> 1   It is impossible to say how first the idea entered my brain; but once conceived, it haunted me day and night. Motive there was none. Passion there was none. I loved the old man. He had never wronged me. He had never given me insult. For his gold I had no desire. I think it was his eye! Yes, it was this! He had the eye of a vulture – a pale blue eye, with a film over it. Whenever it fell upon me, my blood ran cold; and so by degrees – very gradually – I made up my mind to take the life of
> 5   the old man, and thus rid myself of the eye forever.
>
>   Now this is the point. You fancy me mad. Madmen know nothing. But you should have seen me. You should have seen how wisely I proceeded – with what caution – with what foresight I went to work! I was never kinder to the old man than during the whole week before I killed him. And every night, about midnight, I turned the latch of his door and opened it – oh so gently! And then, when I had made an opening sufficient for my head, I put in a dark lantern, all closed, closed, that
> 10   no light shone out, and then I thrust in my head. Oh, you would have laughed to see how cunningly I thrust it in! I moved it slowly – very, very slowly, so that I might not disturb the old man's sleep. It took me an hour to place my whole head within the opening so far that I could see him as he lay upon his bed. Ha! Would a madman have been so wise as this? And then, when my head was well in the room, I undid the lantern cautiously – oh, so cautiously – cautiously (for the hinges creaked) – I undid it just so much that a single thin ray fell upon the vulture eye. And this I did for seven long nights – every
> 15   night just at midnight – but I found the eye always closed; and so it was impossible to do the work; for it was not the old man who vexed me, but his Evil Eye. And every morning, when the day broke, I went boldly into the chamber, and spoke courageously to him, calling him by name in a hearty tone, and inquiring how he has passed the night. So you see he would have been a very clever old man, indeed, to suspect that every night, just at twelve, I looked in upon him while he slept.

Assessment questions

1 What reason does the narrator give for wanting to kill the old man?

_____

_____

2 What does the narrator want the reader to believe about his state of mind? Refer to at least one quotation to support your answer.

_____

_____

_____

3 What does the writer intend the reader to believe about the narrator's state of mind?

_____

_____

Unit 1: Heroes and villains — Section 5 Assessment

4 What impression does the writer give of the character of the old man? Explain your answer below, using quotations from the extract to support your points.

5 Identify three words in the final paragraph that reinforce the idea of the narrator being very careful.

6 Look at the following task and read the student's response that follows.

Task: Write a response to the extract on page 22, considering how the writer has created a suspenseful opening.

> **Response:** Its about someone who wants to kill an old man. He isnt mad because he dos everything very careful and cleverly and he doesnt hate the old man he just worrys about his eye.
> So every night he creeps into the old mans room and hes always asleep so he doesnt kill him and then he just acts like everythings normal the next morning. I think maybe hes mad even thou he says hes not mad.

a What advice would you give to this student to help them improve their response?

b Write your own improved response to the task in the space below.

Section 6
Story structure

In this section, you will practise exploring the purposes of ideas in stories and how they are structured.

Apostrophes

1 Write P or C next to each of these sentences to indicate whether an apostrophe of possession (P) or a contraction (C) is used.

a She's great fun but she can be annoying. _____

b Does anyone know when it's lunchtime? _____

c Children's books are great these days. _____

d Have we decided who's going to the park? _____

e That shirt is not his, it's mine. _____

Ideas and intentions

2 Look again at the summary on page 28 of the Student Book.

a Why does Everard invite Marshall to visit him?
_____
_____

b How does the writer let the reader know that the Brazilian cat is dangerous before Marshall is trapped in its cage?
_____
_____

c Why does the writer choose to do this?
_____
_____

d Before being attacked by the cat, what are Marshall's feelings about Everard?
_____
_____

e Marshall's problem is that he needs money. What obstacles does he face throughout the story?
_____
_____

Unit 1: Heroes and villains — Section 6 Story structure

Set extension activity

3a Make some notes on what Marshall might be thinking and feeling as he travels to Everard's house.

b Now imagine that Marshall has plenty of money already. Write some notes on what he might be thinking and feeling as he travels to Everard's house in these different circumstances.

c Choose which option creates the most interesting scene, and write it up as a section of the story.

d Why did you choose this version? Explain your answer below.

Story structure

4 Look at the notes on page 30 of the Student Book on story structure. The sentences below are a jumbled story outline. Reorder it to complete the table and show which story elements fit into the categories of Exposition, Conflict, Climax and Resolution.

- The mouse meets the monster and is very nearly eaten.
- The mouse meets various creatures who want to eat it.
- The mouse persuades the monster to walk home with him and on the way he finds some food.
- The mouse goes for a walk to look for food.
- The mouse tricks the creatures by pretending to be friends with a monster.

Exposition	
Conflict	
Climax	
Resolution	

5 Complete the story outline below with your own ideas.

Exposition	A poor boy wants to find some gold to help his father.
Conflict	
Climax	The boy fights the dragon and narrowly escapes death.
Resolution	

Unit 1: Heroes and villains — Section 6 Story structure

Set extension activity

6 You are going to plan the structure for your own story about a character who has 24 hours to save the planet.

a Make some notes using the following prompts.

Exposition: What is the main problem, in detail?

_____
_____
_____
_____

Conflict: Who is the villain and how will they try to stop the hero from saving the planet?

_____
_____
_____
_____

Climax: How will the hero and the villain fight it out?

_____
_____
_____
_____

Resolution: How will the hero save the planet?

_____
_____
_____
_____

b Write the opening to your story in the space below. Continue your answer in your notebook if needed.

_____
_____
_____
_____
_____
_____
_____

Section 7
Endings

In this section, you will practise exploring different ways of ending a story.

Story endings

1 Look at this story synopsis.

- A young man from the city buys a house and some land in the countryside. He plans to make a living by growing unusual flowers to sell.
- The locals think he is a fool and they want his plan to fail.
- One old man, who does not like people from the city, secretly diverts the water supply away from the young man's fields.
- At first, things seem to be going well for the young man, but then the flowers shrivel and die.
- The same thing happens the following year.

a Complete the synopsis with your own ending.

_____
_____
_____

b How does your ending make you feel about the characters? Explain your answer below.

_____
_____

2 Look at these other possible endings.

a The old man is trapped in a burning house and is rescued by the young man. The old man admits what he has done, the young man forgives him, and the flower-growing plan is a success.

How does this ending make you feel about the characters? Explain your answer below.

_____
_____
_____

b The young man works so hard that he dies. The old man then learns that the young man was his long-lost son. The old man dies of a broken heart.

How does this ending make you feel about the characters? Explain your answer below.

_____
_____
_____

| Unit 1: Heroes and villains | Section 7 Endings |

Set extension activity

3a Think of a story you know well, from a book or a film, which has a happy ending. Write a summary of the story below.

_____
_____
_____
_____
_____
_____
_____

b Think of a story you know well, from a book or a film, which has a sad ending. Write a summary of the story below.

_____
_____
_____
_____
_____
_____
_____

c Think of a story you know well, from a book or a film, which ends with a surprising twist. Write a summary of the story below.

_____
_____
_____
_____
_____
_____
_____

d Which type of ending do you find most often in the stories you know? Why do you think this is the most common type of ending? Explain your answer below.

_____
_____
_____
_____
_____

Colons and semi-colons

4a Rewrite the following sentences, replacing each conjunction with a colon or a semi-colon.

(i) The young man moves to the countryside because he wants to grow flowers.

(ii) The plan goes wrong when the flowers shrivel and die.

b Rewrite each of the pairs of sentences as one multi-clause sentence, using a colon or semi-colon.

(i) The old man does not like the young man. He does not like people from the city.

(ii) The young man dies. The old man learns the young man was his long-lost son.

Writing endings

5a Write a simple story summary with an ending that will make readers feel happy.

Exposition	
Conflict	
Climax	
Resolution	

b How will this ending make readers feel happy? Explain your answer below.

c Write an alternative ending, designed to make the reader feel sympathy for one of the characters.

d How will this ending make readers feel sympathy for the character? Explain your answer below.

e Which ending do you prefer? Explain your answer below.

Unit 1: Heroes and villains — **Section 7 Endings**

Set extension activity

6 Write a guide explaining how to choose an ending when writing a story. You should cover:
- the different types of ending, with examples
- the different ways endings can make readers feel, with examples.

Section 8
Ways of telling stories

In this section, you will practise exploring different ways of giving the reader information.

Exploring the extract

1 Look again at the extract on page 36 of the Student Book.

a Note down two examples of sentences that give us information about Givens's actions.
___
___

b Note down two examples of sentences that give us information about Josefa's actions.
___
___

c Note down two examples of sentences that give us information about Givens's feelings.
___
___

d Note down two examples of sentences that give us information about Josefa's feelings.
___
___

e Note down two examples of sentences that give us information about what Givens says.
___
___

f Note down two examples of sentences that give us information about what Josefa says.
___
___

2 Write a paragraph, continuing the story from Josefa's point of view. Try to include information or hints about what she can see, what she does, what she says and what she thinks or feels.
___
___
___
___
___

Unit 1: Heroes and villains | **Section 8 Ways of telling stories**

Set extension activity

3a Rewrite the extract on page 36 of the Student Book, so that the story is told from Josefa's point of view. Once again, try to reveal information about:

- what the characters can see
- what they say
- what they do
- what they think or feel.

_____
_____
_____
_____
_____
_____
_____
_____
_____
_____
_____
_____
_____
_____
_____
_____
_____
_____
_____
_____
_____
_____
_____
_____

b Look back over what you have written. Who do we learn most about in your new version, Givens or Josefa? How has telling the story from Josefa's point of view affected who we learn most about? Explain your answer below.

_____
_____
_____
_____
_____
_____

Identifiers

4 Rewrite the conversation below, adding identifiers. Where possible, use precise verbs rather than verbs and adverbs. For example, *she yelled* rather than *she said loudly*.

"It's time to go now," Mum called.
But I'm not ready.
I told you to get ready an hour ago.
Why are you getting angry?
I'm not angry, I'm late.

_____
_____
_____
_____

Telling stories

5 You are going to plan a scene from your own story. Two characters have found a bag full of money and they are staring at it. Make some notes using the following questions as prompts.

a Who are the two characters? What are their names and what are their personalities?
_____
_____
_____

b Where are they and where is the bag of money? Describe the setting.
_____
_____
_____

c What (in detail) do they see when they look at the bag?
_____
_____
_____

d What do they think and feel?
_____
_____
_____

e What do they say to each other?
_____
_____
_____

Set extension activity

6a You are going to write the scene that you planned in **Activity 5**, about two characters who have found a bag of money.

(i) Write one or two sentences using description to set the scene. Describe your characters, where they are and what they are looking at.

_____

_____

_____

(ii) Write one or two sentences using action. For example, what do the characters do?

_____

_____

_____

(iii) Write one or two sentences using speech. You could use these to suggest how the characters feel about each other.

_____

_____

_____

(iv) Write one or two sentences using thoughts. You could use these to suggest what the characters think is going to happen.

_____

_____

_____

b Write two paragraphs of your scene in the space below. You could use some of the sentences you have written in the activities above, or you could write new sentences. Continue your answer in your notebook if needed.

_____

_____

_____

_____

_____

_____

_____

Section 9
Structuring sentences

In this section, you will practise exploring sentence structure choices and their impact on the reader.

Exploring short sentences

1 Look at lines 43–48 of the extract on page 40 of the Student Book and then answer the questions that follow.

a Do the short sentences suggest the words are spoken quickly or slowly? Explain your answer below.

_____
_____
_____

b Henrietta speaks in extremely short sentences. What does this suggest about her? For example, *She is kind/rude/indecisive*. Explain your answer below.

_____
_____
_____

c Now look at these two versions of the same sentence.

   (i) "Who cares?" said Henrietta, laughing.
   (ii) "Who cares that I stole from them?" said Henrietta, laughing nastily as if it was the biggest joke in the world.

Which version of the sentence more effectively creates the sense of Henrietta not caring? Explain your answer below.

_____
_____
_____

Exploring longer sentences

2 Read this longer, multi-clause sentence from the extract on page 40 of the Student Book.

> She chained her arms around the rider's waist, and, after some restraint, grabbed hold of the controls and steered the bike down the street.

Rewrite the sentence as three single-clause sentences.

_____
_____
_____

Unit 1: Heroes and villains | **Section 9 Structuring sentences**

Set extension activity

3a Look again at the extract on page 40 of the Student Book. Rewrite the part of the extract that describes the conversation between Ella and Henrietta. Use long sentences and add as much descriptive detail as you can imagine to create a clear picture of the scene, and to describe how the characters speak, look and feel. Continue your answer in your notebook if needed.

b What are the advantages of using longer sentences with more descriptive detail?

c What are the advantages of using short sentences to describe a tense conversation?

Adverbials

4 Rewrite the sentences below, linking them by adding an adverbial at the start of all but the first sentence.

a I got dressed. I packed my bags. I waved goodbye to my parents.

b The water was cold. I really wanted to get in and join my friends.

Building sentences

5 Look at these single-clause sentences.

I screamed. I raced downstairs. I tore open the front door.

a Rewrite them as one multi-clause sentence, linking the clauses with a comma and the conjunction *and*.

b Now rewrite them using two conjunctions other than *and*.

6 Read this paragraph and then answer the questions that follow.

I gripped the branch tightly. I walked my feet up the trunk. I pulled myself up onto the next branch. I realised I was high enough off the ground to break a leg if I fell. It started to rain. The branch was really slippery. I started to panic.

a Rewrite the paragraph, using longer multi-clause sentences. Try to use as few sentences as possible. Link clauses and sentences with conjunctions and adverbials as appropriate.

b Now rewrite the paragraph again, using a mixture of short sentences and longer multi-clause sentences. Use appropriate punctuation or conjunctions to link clauses, and adverbials to link some of the sentences.

Unit 1: Heroes and villains | **Section 9 Structuring sentences**

Set extension activity

7a You are going to write a scene from a story in which the narrator heroically tries to rescue a person or animal from a dangerous situation. Make some notes using the following prompts.

(i) Who or what is being rescued? What is the danger?

_____

_____

(ii) Describe the moment when the hero realises they must act. What do they see, smell or hear? What do they feel?

_____

_____

_____

_____

(iii) Describe what the hero does to rescue the person or animal.

_____

_____

_____

_____

b Now write the scene, thinking carefully about how to link your sentences and paragraphs, and about when to use short and longer sentences.

_____

_____

_____

_____

_____

_____

_____

_____

_____

_____

Section 10
Reviewing, revising and proofreading

This section links to pages 44–47 of the Student Book.

In this section, you will develop your skills in checking the accuracy and effectiveness of your writing.

Homophones

1 Underline any errors in the sentences below.

a I'll have too of the red ones please, and too of the green ones too.

b Their it is! That's their car!

c No, no, no! You can't do that, you no.

d If you stand over hear by the window you can hear the birds.

Irregular past tenses

2 Rewrite the following sentences in the past tense. Pay careful attention to the spelling of the past tense form of the verb.

a I sleep for hours.

b I remember nothing when I wake up.

c I try to remember how I come to be in a barn.

d I think about my sister and begin to remember.

e Is it her who brings me here?

f I stand up and my head spins.

g Outside, the sun breaks through the clouds.

Unit 1: Heroes and villains — Section 10 Reviewing, revising and proofreading

Set extension activity

3 Write a one-page worksheet for students, helping them to revise the skill of proofreading. Use the prompts below.

a A reminder of common homophones

b A reminder of irregular past-tense verb forms

c A paragraph of sample text for students to correct (including lots of misspelt homophones and incorrect past-tense verb forms)

d The same paragraph written for **Activity 3c** but without any errors, so that students can check their answers

Reviewing vocabulary

4 Look at the sentences below. Rewrite them, replacing the underlined verbs with more powerful, dramatic synonyms.

a I was shocked. 'No way!' I said.

b It was going to be close but I had to make it. I ran towards the train doors.

c 'Please don't hurt me,' he said.

d The glass broke into a thousand pieces.

e She held the handlebars with all her strength.

Reviewing sentence structure

5 Read this short text.

I knocked at the door and waited with bated breath but there was no reply.
I knocked again. Inside I heard a deep growl.
Heavy footsteps grew louder. Something approached the door.
I raised my sword. I waited.
Slowly, the door creaked open.

a Rewrite the first sentence as two shorter sentences.

b Rewrite the two sentences beginning 'Heavy' and 'Something' as one multi-clause sentence.

c Rewrite the whole text, choosing sentence structures that make it sound as tense and dramatic as possible.

Set extension activity

6 Revise the skills you have covered in the second half of this unit, ready for the assessment in the next lesson. You may find it helpful to note down the key points covered in each of the sections so far. If there are any areas where you do not feel confident, reread the information given in the Student Book throughout this unit. Think back to when you planned for the previous assessment. What helped? What could you improve on?

Section 6: Story structure

Apostrophes of contraction show that some letters have been missed out.

Section 7: Endings

Section 8: Ways of telling stories

Section 9: Structuring sentences

Section 10: Reviewing, revising and proofreading

Section 11
Assessment

This section links to pages 48–49 of the Student Book.

In this section, you will identify the mistakes in a sample response from a student and write an improved version.

1 Look at the following task and read the student's response that follows.

Task: Write a story featuring a hero and a villain. Neither should be defeated and the story should have a cliffhanger ending.

Response: Mrs Gory had a nasty look. Her dog looks nasty as well. It had saliva dripping out of its nasty mouth and it looked at me like it wants to eat me because it probably does.

She was angry because my football had gone in her garden. She says she saw me climbing over the fence to get it. Last time she warned me. She says shed set the dog on me if I do it again

so here we are on the street outside her house and I've got my football under my arm and she had the dog with her.

I find a stick on the ground so I give it to the dog before she can let it go and the dog chews on it. I tell her goodbye and walk away and she shouts at me.

When I looked back down the street shes gone away so that was good

You are going to improve and extend this response.
  a Underline any spelling or punctuation mistakes.
  b Underline any verbs that are in the wrong tense.
  c Write a 'V' next to any opportunities to improve the impact of the writing by making different vocabulary choices.
  d Write an 'S' next to any opportunities to improve the impact of the writing by varying sentence length and structure.
  e Use the space in the box below to make some notes and plan how you will improve this answer. Think in particular about story structure and ways of revealing information.

Unit 1: Heroes and villains — Section 11 Assessment

2 Rewrite your improved version of the answer in the space below. Remember to:
- create a villain
- show the reader elements of the characters' personalities
- use different ways of revealing information
- follow the four-part story structure you have learned
- end with a cliffhanger.

Section 1
Spotting persuasive techniques

In this section, you will practise identifying key points of information and vocabulary choices the writer has used to persuade you.

Identifying key information

1 Look again at the poster on page 52 of the Student Book.

a Copy two sentences from the poster that summarise the message the writer is trying to get across.
_____
_____

b In what circumstances is it important to drink more than two pints of water per day?
_____

c What does the writer suggest is the best source of drinking water?
_____

Combining key points

2a According to the poster, which are the best alternatives to drinking tap water?
_____

b Which alternatives to drinking tap water are not good for you?
_____

c What are the benefits of tap water as opposed to the alternatives mentioned in the poster?
_____
_____
_____

3 Write two or three sentences that combine and summarise the writer's view of tap water and alternative sources of water.
_____
_____
_____
_____

Unit 2: Safe and sound — Section 1 Spotting persuasive techniques

Set extension activity

4 You have been asked to write a persuasive leaflet designed to convince people to eat more fruit and vegetables.

a Research and note down everything you can find out about the benefits to the body of eating more fruit and vegetables.

_____

b Research and note down everything you can find out about the benefits to the environment of people eating more fruit and vegetables and less meat and processed food.

_____

Imperative verbs

5 Rewrite each of the following sentences using imperative verbs. An example is provided.
You should eat more vegetables.
Imperative: *Eat more vegetables!*

a I suggest you hurry up.

Imperative: _____

b Calling an ambulance might help.

Imperative: _____

c You are going to school.

Imperative: _____

Vocabulary choices

6 Look at the extract from the poster below and copy out one sentence that contains the following.

> **Drink at least 2 pints of water every day.**
> Drink more when it's hot, or if you're exercising, playing sport, dancing, or on a long flight.
> The best source of water is your tap.
> Tap water contains useful minerals, such as calcium and magnesium.
> Bottled waters are unlikely to be better for you than tap water.

a Positive vocabulary: _____

b Negative vocabulary: _____

c An imperative verb: _____

Parts of speech

7 Look at the extract below and complete the table to list all the nouns, adjectives and verbs.

> Isotonic sports drinks and fancy fizzes are not as good for you as water. Even if they don't contain much sugar (and many do), they're very acid and can damage your teeth by eating into the enamel.

Nouns	Adjectives	Verbs

Unit 2: Safe and sound — Section 1 Spotting persuasive techniques

Set extension activity

8a Continue planning your leaflet. Look back at the notes you made for **Activity 4** and then complete the tables below. Examples are provided.

(i) Good for the body

Positive vocabulary	Negative vocabulary	Imperative verbs
Nutritious	Illness	Choose more...

(ii) Good for the environment

Positive vocabulary	Negative vocabulary	Imperative verbs
Cleaner	Cows pollute	Help save...

b Now write your persuasive leaflet in the space below. Continue your answer in your notebook if needed.

Section 2
Persuasive vocabulary

In this section, you will practise exploring further how writers' choices of ideas and language can make a text more persuasive.

Identifying key ideas

1 Look again at the webpage on page 56 of the Student Book and answer the following questions.

a In your own words, summarise how sugar is bad for your teeth.
_____
_____

b Which types of food and drink does the webpage suggest do not damage your teeth?
_____
_____

2 Write two sentences summarising what the whole webpage says that you should and should not do.
_____
_____
_____
_____

Inferring ideas

3 Contained in each of the following sentences is an implied message about something you should not do. Rewrite each sentence so that it reads as an explicit warning not to do something.

a It may be safer to walk on the pavement.
_____

b Crossing busy roads anywhere other than at crossings with traffic lights can be dangerous.
_____
_____

c Cycling on pavements can lead to accidents.
_____

d Be aware that these animals can bite you if you feed them.
_____

Unit 2: Safe and sound — Section 2 Persuasive vocabulary

Set extension activity

4 Look again at the webpage on page 56 of the Student Book.

a Identify the positive messages where the writer is suggesting what you should do rather than what you should not do. Rewrite three of these positive messages as negative warnings about what not to do.

b Rewrite the whole webpage using only negative points and warnings about what not to do. Continue your answer in your notebook if needed.

c Compare the version you have written with the original. Which do you think is more persuasive? Explain your answer below.

Connotations

5 Read this extract from the webpage on page 56 of the Student Book and answer the questions.

> An attractive and healthy smile is important. It can boost your confidence and help you feel good about yourself.

> If you don't look after your teeth and gums properly you could suffer from a number of different conditions that will make you stand out from the crowd – for all the wrong reasons:
> - Bad breath
> - Stained teeth
> - Tooth decay
> - Gum disease
> - Tooth loss
> - Dental erosion

a From the text above, note down all the words that have positive and negative connotations.

Positive connotations	Negative connotations

b Choose the word that you feel has the most powerfully positive connotations. What are the specific connotations of this word? Explain your choice below.

_____

_____

c Choose the word that you feel has the most powerfully negative connotations. What are the specific connotations of this word? Explain your choice below.

_____

_____

Writing persuasively

6a Write one sentence using vocabulary with very positive connotations, suggesting that the reader should try a particular activity. For example, a sport or an entertainment experience.

_____

_____

b Write one sentence using vocabulary with very negative connotations, warning the reader that something is dangerous.

_____

_____

Unit 2: Safe and sound — Section 2 Persuasive vocabulary

Set extension activity

7 You are going to write a text warning readers of the dangers they face online.

a Make some notes using the following prompts.

(i) What dangers should people be aware of?

(ii) What should they do to stay safe?

(iii) What benefits can people enjoy if they avoid the dangers?

b Now write your text, choosing the most powerful vocabulary, with positive and negative connotations as appropriate. It may help to structure your writing using three paragraphs, one for each topic covered in **Activity 7a** above. Continue your answer in your notebook if needed.

Section 3
Responding to a text

In this section, you will practise your skills in responding to texts.

Identifying intention and audience

1 Look at the three extracts below from information texts and answer the questions for each one.

Before you go to secondary school, there are some things you need to know.

a Who is the intended audience?
___

b How do you know?
___

There are some important safety guidelines to be aware of when you use the trampoline park.

c What is the purpose of this text?
___

d How do you know?
___

As you already know, growing fruit trees takes time.

e Who is the intended audience?
___

f How do you know?
___

2 Look back at the poster about drinking water on page 52 of the Student Book.

a Who is the intended audience?
___

b How do you know?
___

c What is the purpose of the poster?
___

Unit 2: Safe and sound — Section 3 Responding to a text

Set extension activity

3 Look again at the poster about drinking water on page 52 of the Student Book.

a Make some notes explaining how you would change the text of the poster if your intended audience were only people over the age of 60.

b Make some notes explaining how you would change the text if your intended audience were eight-year-old children.

c Choose one of these new audiences (people over the age of 60 or eight-year-old children). Rewrite the text of the poster for this new audience. Continue your answer in your notebook if needed.

Quotations

4 The following sentences include embedded quotations, shown in italics. Rewrite them, punctuating them correctly.

a The writer says that there are often age restrictions *you need to be at least 13 to sign up.*

_____

b The writer suggests that *if you are being bullied you should report it.*

_____

c The writer states that until you know how to use social media sites *safely*, you should stay away from them.

_____
_____

5 Look again at this extract from the webpage on page 60 of the Student Book.

> Once you've put something online you've lost control of it – it can be copied, shared or edited. It could turn up anywhere. You might be happy showing a funny picture to your friends but would you want your parents or teachers to see it?

a Write down one quotation from the extract that states the risk.

_____

b Write down one quotation from the extract that suggests potential negative consequences.

_____

c Write one or two sentences, with your quotations embedded, explaining the point that the writer is making.

_____
_____
_____

Vocabulary

6 Summarise the point the writer is making in the extract below from the webpage, referring to at least two of the following words and embedding them in your answer:

limit | share | trust | privacy

> Most social networks let you limit what you share to friends or followers you've OKed. It's always a good idea to let only people you know and trust see your stuff. Learn how to use privacy settings and how to block people who are bothering you.

_____
_____
_____

Set extension activity

7 Find a text that includes safety guidelines or recommendations. For example, you could choose road safety or health advice online. Make some notes using the prompts below.

a In one sentence, summarise what the writer is trying to persuade you to think or do.

b What are the key reasons the writer gives to persuade you?

c What vocabulary has the writer used that has particularly strong connotations?

d Write one or two paragraphs explaining what the writer is trying to achieve, and how they have achieved it. Remember to use relevant quotations.

e Look back over what you have written and correct any mistakes. Pay particular attention to the punctuation you have used with embedded quotations.

Section 4
Organising your response

In this section, you will practise exploring ways of organising a response to a text.

Identifying intentions

1 Look again at the webpage on page 64 of the Student Book. In one sentence, summarise its key purpose or intention.

_____

_____

2 List three main areas of danger that the writer wants parents to be aware of.

a _____ b _____ c _____

Choosing evidence

3 Find a short quotation from the webpage on page 64 of the Student Book to support each statement.

a The writer refers to statistics to support some of the points made.

_____

b The writer uses imperative verbs when offering advice on what to do.

_____

c The writer suggests that babies and young children are more likely to seriously injure themselves by falling than in any other way.

_____

d The writer suggests that children's curiosity puts them at risk.

_____

4 What is the writer intending to do other than to warn about danger? Explain your answer below, using quotations from the webpage.

_____

_____

_____

_____

Unit 2: Safe and sound — Section 4 Organising your response

Set extension activity

5 You have been asked to write a worksheet for students to help them practise choosing evidence.

a Write a sentence or two explaining why it is important to use quotations when responding to a text.

_____
_____
_____

b Write a sentence or two summarising how to choose the best evidence to support a point.

_____
_____
_____

c As an example, write one point about the webpage on page 64 of the Student Book, using a suitable quotation as evidence.

_____
_____
_____

d Write down five statements about the webpage that students using your worksheet will be asked to find evidence for.

(i) _____
(ii) _____
(iii) _____
(iv) _____
(v) _____

e For an answer sheet, write down as many quotations as you can find that could be used to support each statement.

(i) _____
_____

(ii) _____
_____

(iii) _____
_____

(iv) _____
_____

(v) _____
_____

Structuring your paragraphs

6 Write a paragraph around the following statement: The writer of the webpage on page 64 of the Student Book uses statistics to persuade the reader that the dangers are serious.

Remember to include a key point, evidence and an explanation.

_____

_____

_____

_____

_____

_____

Vocabulary choices

7 Reread this section from the webpage and answer the following questions.

> **Hazards around the home**
> Statistics have shown that the most common place for babies and young children to be injured, often seriously, is at home. Children aged 0–4 years old are most at risk from hazards in the home because they spend a lot of time there, before starting school, and are curious to explore their surroundings.
>
> So, what can we do to protect children in our care from some everyday, but often extremely dangerous, home hazards? The type and number of potential dangers will vary from home to home, but here are some tips to help you make your home safer for little ones.

a Note down every word or phrase that you feel is evidence of the writer trying to evoke a powerful emotional response.

_____

_____

b Which one of these emotive words or phrases would you choose as an alternative one-word heading for this section? Explain your answer below.

_____

_____

_____

_____

_____

8 Complete the following sentence:

Using emotive vocabulary such as _____,

the writer intends to engage parents who want to _____

_____

Unit 2: Safe and sound — Section 4 Organising your response

Set extension activity

9 Revise the skills you have covered in the first half of this unit, ready for the assessment in the next lesson. You may find it helpful to note down the key points covered in each of the sections so far. If there are any areas where you do not feel confident, reread the appropriate pages in the Student Book.

Section 1: Spotting persuasive techniques

When first looking at a text, try to identify the writer's intention and key ideas.

Section 2: Persuasive vocabulary

Section 3: Responding to a text

Section 4: Organising your response

Section 5
Assessment

This section links to pages 68–69 of the Student Book.

In this section, you will answer questions on a short extract and improve a sample response from a student.

The extract below is an information poster about water safety.

▼ **Read the poster and then answer the questions that follow it.**

SUN, SEA, SAFETY

1   A day at the beach is fun for all the family, so it's easy to forget that there are real dangers for you and your children to be aware of. Around the world, more than one million people lose their lives each year due to drowning, and the majority of cases are in open water, including the sea. Do you want to avoid being one of them? Here are the top things you need to know to help you and your loved ones stay safe at the beach.

5   • **Inflatable dinghies and floats** – if you use these in the open sea they can kill you. Lots of people have drowned after being carried out to sea on inflatables by the tide. If you want to enjoy inflatable dinghies and floats, use them in safe, sheltered water such as large rock pools.

   • **Cold water** can be deadly as it can send your body into shock and prevent you from being able to swim properly, leading to drowning. Anything under 15 degrees is classed as cold water. When swimming in seas with a cold
10   temperature, stay close to the shore, don't stay in the sea for too long, and think about wearing a wetsuit to keep your body temperature comfortable.

   • **Rip tides** are lethal. These are currents of water that flow away from the beach and out to sea. If you try to swim straight back to the beach against a rip tide, you will use up all your energy and end up being carried far out to sea. If you do get caught in a rip tide, the best thing you can do is to swim sideways, parallel to the beach, until you are
15   free of the rip. Then you can swim back to shore.

   Finally, although you should always assess the risks yourself, it is much safer to swim at a beach that is patrolled by lifeguards who can reach you and your family if you get into trouble. Some beaches also display flags to indicate the safest places for swimming.

   So remember to be really careful with inflatables, cold water and rip tides, and only swim between the flags on
20   lifeguard-patrolled beaches.

   Play hard, play happy, play safe!

Assessment questions

1 Who is the intended audience for this poster? Support your answer with a quotation from it.
_____

2 How many people drown each year around the world? _____

3 Why are inflatable dinghies and floats dangerous?
_____
_____

Unit 2: Safe and sound **Section 5 Assessment**

4 Write down one example of emotive language in the first paragraph and explain what response the writer is trying to create.

_____
_____
_____

5 Look at the following question and read the student's response that follows.

> **Question:** How persuasive is this text?

> **Response:** Its about how to stay safe at the beach because lots of people can drown every year about 1 million people do and lots of them are children. Theres three things that can kill you at the beach. Theirs playing with inflatable dinghies and floats which is weird because I think it would be good to have a float in the sea not dangerous but that's what it says.
>
> As well you've got to be careful about getting too cold because it can mean you don't swim properly and then you've got to be careful about tides which sometimes sucked people out to sea and then they couldn't get back but its ok if theres lifeguards who can come and save you so go to beaches where theirs lifeguards.

a What advice would you give to the student to help them improve their response?

_____
_____
_____
_____
_____

b Write your own response to the question in the space below. Continue your answer in your notebook if needed.

_____
_____
_____
_____
_____
_____
_____
_____
_____

Section 6
Persuasive paragraphs

In this section, you will practise exploring paragraph structure in a persuasive instruction text.

Structuring paragraphs

1 Look at the second section of the webpage on page 70 of the Student Book: *What is fake news?*

a What is the key point?
_____

b What evidence or examples are provided?
_____

2 Look at the final section of the webpage entitled *Fake or real?*

a What is the key point?
_____

b Explain why you think that the writer has not included examples or evidence in this section.
_____
_____

Paragraphing persuasive texts

3 Which section of the webpage states the writer's opinion most persuasively? Explain your answer below. Use embedded quotations if possible.
_____
_____
_____

4 Which of the following statements do you most agree with?
A In a persuasive text, each paragraph should contain a key point, evidence or examples, and a suggestion about how the reader should change their opinions or actions.
B A persuasive text should contain key points, evidence or examples, and suggestions about how the reader should change their opinions or actions.
Explain your answer below. Continue your answer in your notebook if needed.
_____
_____
_____

Unit 2: Safe and sound — Section 6 Persuasive paragraphs

Set extension activity

5a Rewrite the webpage on page 70 of the Student Book so that every section includes a clear key point, examples or evidence, and a suggestion about how the reader should change their actions or opinions. You can make up examples or evidence if that is easier. An example is provided. Continue your answer in your notebook if needed.

Original: We all like to share news stories with our friends on social media, but do any of us check if the stories are actually true?

Rewritten: Lots of news stories we see on social media are untrue. Evidence suggests that up to 50 per cent of the stories posted are made up, and we should check whether they are true before we share them.

b Which version of the webpage – the original or your rewritten version – do you think is the most persuasive? Explain your answer below.

Demonstrative pronouns

6a Look at the following sentences.
(i) We went swimming this afternoon. It was great fun.
What does *It* refer to?

_____

(ii) My sister keeps hiding my things. She is really annoying.
What does *She* refer to?

_____

b Rewrite these pairs of sentences using a pronoun in the second sentence.
(i) Max is a dog. Max is really energetic.

_____

(ii) You must wear a bike helmet. A bike helmet will keep you safe.

_____

Writing persuasive paragraphs

7 You have been asked to write a persuasive text about how students should respond to bullying.

a Note down some ideas about why it is an important issue, the types of bullying students might encounter, and what you think they should do about it.

_____
_____
_____
_____
_____

b Now write a paragraph of your text. Continue your answer in your notebook if needed.
Try to include:
- one key point
- evidence or examples
- suggestions about how students should change their opinions or actions
- imperative verbs.

_____
_____
_____
_____
_____

Set extension activity

8 You are going to write a persuasive text explaining why readers should learn to write persuasively, including tips on how to do so effectively.

a Note down some ideas using the following prompts:
 (i) Why is it useful to be able to write persuasively?

(ii) How should readers write persuasively?

(iii) What are some examples of how persuasive writing can be used?

b Write your guide in the space below.

Section 7
Persuasive structures

In this section, you will practise exploring the structure of a persuasive text.

Key information

1a Look again at the webpage on page 74 of the Student Book. In your own words, define 'mental wellbeing'.

_____

_____

b Note down three things you are able to do if your mental wellbeing is good.

_____

_____

Text structure and features

2 For each feature below, write a few sentences explaining its purpose and where the feature should go in the structure of the text.

a Heading or title

_____

_____

b Introduction

_____

_____

c Subheadings

_____

_____

d Paragraphs

_____

_____

e Bulleted lists

_____

_____

Unit 2: Safe and sound — Section 7 Persuasive structures

Set extension activity

3 You are going to gather information and ideas to include in a text that you will write in the next set extension activity. The subject you will cover is: How to stay safe when travelling to and from school. Use the prompts below to gather information and plan your text.

a What are the common ways that students travel to school?

b What dangers should students be aware of when travelling to school?

c What precautions would help students to limit the dangers?

d Suggest two or three possible headings for your text.

e Write down some ideas for subheadings under which you could group your points.

f Note down any words or phrases that you think your audience might find particularly powerful.

Determiners

4 Rewrite these sentences, replacing the underlined determiners to make the meaning clearer.

a A woman stood up. <u>A</u> woman walked to the front of the bus.

___

b Cats and dogs are popular pets. <u>Some</u> animals do not always feel comfortable around each other.

___

c A man bought some new shoes. <u>A man's</u> old shoes had holes in them.

___

Responding to the text

5a Complete the table with examples from the webpage on page 74 of the Student Book.

Positive language	Negative language	Imperative verbs
confident	stresses	Think about…

b For each category of the table in **Activity 5a**, write a short paragraph explaining how the writer uses language to persuade. Remember to include examples from the webpage as evidence.

Positive language:
___
___
___
___

Negative language:
___
___
___
___

Imperative verbs:
___
___
___

Set extension activity

6 You are going to write a persuasive text on the subject of how to stay safe while travelling to and from school, using the structural features explored in **Activities 3 to 5**. Remember to include a heading, an introduction, subheadings, paragraphs and bulleted lists if appropriate. Your audience is new school students, and you should remember that the purpose of the text is to inform and persuade. Create your text in the space below. Continue your answer in your notebook if needed.

Section 8
Exploring the writer's choices

In this section, you will practise exploring how the writer's choices of ideas, vocabulary and sentence structure can make texts more persuasive.

Identifying persuasive ideas

1a Note down three negative consequences of lack of sleep mentioned in the webpage on page 78 of the Student Book.

(i) _____

(ii) _____

(iii) _____

b 'Getting a good night's sleep can help you to cope better with the stresses of life.' What negative consequence of lack of sleep is implied by this statement?

_____

Emotive language

2a Rewrite each of the following sentences from the webpage using more powerful, emotive language.

(i) Sleep deprivation can make it hard to concentrate and remember things – the last thing you need when you are in an exam situation.

_____
_____

(ii) Getting a good night's sleep can help you to cope better with the stresses of life.

_____
_____

b Why do you think the writer has chosen to use emotive language in a few but not all the points they make? Explain your answer below. Continue your answer in your notebook if needed.

_____
_____
_____

Unit 2: Safe and sound
Section 8 Exploring the writer's choices
73

Set extension activity

3a Rewrite the whole webpage on page 78 of the Student Book, using powerful emotive language in every possible sentence. Continue your answer in your notebook if needed.

b Which version – the original or your rewritten text – do you think is more persuasive? Explain your answer below.

Sentence types

4a Write down three single-clause sentences of your own.

_____
_____
_____

b Write down three multi-clause sentences of your own.

_____
_____
_____

c Circle the main clauses and underline the subordinate clauses in each of the following sentences.

(i) I was tired but I was safe.

(ii) I was tired because I had been running.

(iii) I was tired so I fell asleep.

d Look back at the three sentences in **Activity 4c**.
(i) Write down any co-ordinating conjunctions.

_____

(ii) Write down any subordinating conjunctions.

_____

Developing a response using evidence

5 You are going to develop a response to the webpage 'Teens' teeth' on page 56 of the Student Book. The question you will answer is: How does the writer persuade you to look after your teeth?

Read through the webpage and identify a quotation that you find particularly persuasive. Note down the key point that the quotation is making. Finally, write a short explanation of how the writer has used the quotation to be persuasive. Use the prompts below to structure your points.

Quotation

_____
_____

Key point

_____
_____

Explanation

_____
_____

Unit 2: Safe and sound — Section 8 Exploring the writer's choices

Set extension activity

6 Continue to plan your response to the question: How does the writer of 'Teens' teeth' persuade you to look after your teeth?

a Identify two more quotations and complete the paragraph plans below.

Quotation 1

Key point

Explanation

Quotation 2

Key point

Explanation

b In two or three paragraphs, write your response to the question. Continue your answer in your notebook.

Section 9
Rhetorical devices

In this section, you will practise exploring how a variety of rhetorical devices can make a text more persuasive.

Identifying rhetorical devices

1 Read through this text and answer the questions that follow.

> 1 **On your bike!**
> Travelling by car, train and aeroplane can be convenient but it is no good for your body and could be catastrophic for the environment. What is the best alternative? The humble bicycle.
>
> People who cycle to school or work typically do more than ten times as much exercise as those who sit in a motorised
> 5 vehicle. That's why millions of people are switching over, or switching back, to cycling.
>
> **Stay safe, happy and active!**
> Of course, there are some safety precautions you need to take on the road. A good cycling road awareness course is cheap and gives you all the training you need to stay safe. Wearing a helmet is a must. And wearing high-visibility clothing is a good idea too. Most of all, keep your wits about you and use your senses to make sure you don't put yourself
> 10 in harm's way on the road. Use your eyes, use your ears, use your brain!

a Write down one example from the text above of each of the following rhetorical devices.

Rhetorical device	Example
Rhetorical question	
Triple structure	
Repetition	
List	
Direct address	

b Come up with a rhetorical question that could be used as a title for the text.

_____

2 What is the benefit of using direct address in a persuasive text? Explain your answer below.

_____
_____
_____
_____

Unit 2: Safe and sound — Section 9 Rhetorical devices

Set extension activity

3 You have been asked by your local leisure centre to write a page for their website, designed to persuade people to take up swimming. Make some notes in preparation, using the prompts below.

a Why is it important or beneficial to know how to swim?

b How do you learn to swim?

c What are the health benefits of swimming?

d What are the other benefits of swimming?

Exploring rhetorical devices

4 Look back at the examples of rhetorical devices that you noted down in **Activity 1** on page 76 of this Workbook. For each one, write a sentence or two, including the quotation, explaining the effect of that rhetorical device. An example is provided.

> **Rhetorical question:** The writer uses a rhetorical question: 'What is the best alternative?' This effectively highlights the writer's main argument in the first part of the text: that the bike is the best mode of transport.

a Triple structure: _____

b Repetition: _____

c List: _____

d Direct address: _____

Creating your own rhetorical devices

5 Look back at the notes you made for **Activity 3**. Create two examples of each of the following rhetorical devices that you could use in your persuasive text about swimming.

a Rhetorical question: _____

b Triple structure: _____

c Repetition: _____

d List: _____

e Direct address: _____

Unit 2: Safe and sound — Section 9 Rhetorical devices

Set extension activity

6 You are going to write your persuasive text, designed to persuade people to take up swimming. Look back at the notes you have made for **Activities 3 and 5** on pages 77 and 78 of this Workbook. Try to include:
- a title
- at least three headings
- examples of each of the rhetorical devices you have explored.

Write your text below. Continue your answer in your notebook if needed.

Section 10
Getting ready to respond

In this section, you will develop your skills in identifying relevant features of a text and planning your response to it.

Reread the **SUN, SEA, SAFETY** poster on page 62 of this Workbook and complete these activities.

Structure

1a Place a tick next to each of the following structural features that the writer has used.

- heading ☐
- introduction ☐
- subheadings ☐
- paragraphs ☐
- bulleted list ☐

b Which feature helps the writer explain the risks most powerfully? Explain your answer below.

_____
_____

c Which section of the poster establishes the writer's intention and the intended audience?

_____
_____

Vocabulary and intention

2a Write down any examples you can find in the poster of emotive vocabulary with connotations of danger and death.

_____

b In one sentence, summarise what you think the writer is trying to achieve by using this vocabulary.

_____
_____

c Write down any examples of emotive vocabulary linked to caring for and protecting children.

_____

d In one sentence, summarise what you think the writer is trying to achieve by using this vocabulary.

_____
_____

Unit 2: Safe and sound — Section 10 Getting ready to respond

Set extension activity

3 Look again at the **SUN, SEA, SAFETY** poster on page 62 of this Workbook, as well as the answers you wrote for **Activities 1 and 2**, and then answer the following questions.

a How does the structure of the poster help the writer achieve their intention?

_____
_____
_____
_____
_____
_____
_____
_____
_____
_____
_____
_____
_____
_____

b How do the writer's vocabulary choices help them achieve their intention?

_____
_____
_____
_____
_____
_____
_____
_____
_____
_____
_____

Rhetorical devices

4 Look again at the **SUN, SEA, SAFETY** poster on page 62 of this Workbook and write down one example of each of these rhetorical devices.

Rhetorical device	Example
Rhetorical question	
Triple structure	
Repetition	
List	
Direct address	

5 For each rhetorical device example selected for **Activity 4**, write a key point and explanation of how it helps the writer achieve their intention.

a Rhetorical question

_____

_____

b Triple structure

_____

_____

c Repetition

_____

_____

d List

_____

_____

e Direct address

_____

_____

6 Which rhetorical device used in the **SUN, SEA, SAFETY** poster do you find the most powerful? Explain your answer below.

_____

_____

_____

_____

Set extension activity

7 Revise the skills you have covered in the second half of this unit, ready for the assessment in the next lesson. You may find it helpful to note down the key points covered in each of the sections so far. If there are any areas where you do not feel confident, reread the information given in the Student Book throughout this unit. Think back to when you planned for the previous assessment. What helped? What could you improve on?

Section 6: Persuasive paragraphs

Look at the title and first line of a text to find out its intention and target audience.

Section 7: Persuasive structures

Section 8: Exploring the writer's choices

Section 9: Rhetorical devices

Section 10: Getting ready to respond

Section 11
Assessment

This section links to pages 90–91 of the Student Book.

In this section, you will identify the mistakes in a sample response from a student and write an improved version.

The extract below is from an article about the health benefits of taking a break from sitting.

▼ **Read the extract and then answer the questions that follow it.**

---

1   **Stand up for yourself!**
   Did you know that sitting down for more than four hours per day leads to life-threatening health problems?

   That's right, simply sitting down too much can increase the risk of killers like cancer, dementia, depression, diabetes, heart disease and obesity.

5   Why? Because if you spend too long sitting down:
   - Enzymes slow down instead of burning harmful blood fats – these then stay in your system.
   - You burn fewer calories, leading to weight gain.
   - Your blood pressure and insulin levels increase.

   What should you do?
10 You might think that sitting down is what we all do most of the time – but it needn't be. Here are some things you should do to reduce the amount of time you spend on the sofa:
   - Walk or cycle to work or school – or at least some of the way.
   - Take some exercise at break and lunch times during the day.
   - Stand up and walk around the office or classroom whenever you can (if you're allowed to).
15 - Ask your boss or your teacher if you can have a 'standing desk'. They're the same as normal desks – just higher so you stand at them instead of sitting behind them.

   Our lifestyles involve far too much sitting around and far too little movement. It's a massive problem but you can do something about it today. Get up, stand up, wake up! The time to act is now!

---

1 Look at the following question and read the student's response that follows.

Question: How does the writer persuade the reader to stand up more?

Response: This text was about how standing up was impourtant and better for you than siting down. Their were lots of reesons why sitting down is bad for you like it can gave you hart disease and other things because of not standing up enouh and we should all do more exercise witch is really important. We can do more standing up by doing things like walking to school and standing up in lesons. I think its really impourtant we all do this and then we can live longer because its easy to change our lives and stand up more and sit down less.

Unit 2: Safe and sound — Section 11 Assessment

You are going to improve and extend this response.

a Underline any spelling or punctuation mistakes.
b Underline any verbs that are in the wrong tense.
c Write an 'E' next to any opportunities to add evidence.
d Write an 'S' next to any opportunities to improve the impact of the writing by varying sentence length and structure.
e Write a 'P' wherever you think paragraph breaks should be added.
f Use the space below to make some notes and plan how you will improve this answer.

2 Rewrite your improved version of the answer below. You should write two or three paragraphs. Continue your answer in your notebook if needed. Remember to:

- Address what the writer does to persuade the reader.
- Use quotations from the text to support the points you make.
- Mention specific rhetorical devices and explain why they are effective.

Section 1
Exploring a fictional future

In this section, you will practise exploring how writers can engage their readers in an imaginary world.

Summarising key ideas

1 Look again at the extract on page 94 of the Student Book.

a What do we learn about the New Society and its rules? Read through the extract and note down all the information that is stated or implied about the New Society.

_____
_____
_____
_____

b Summarise the information you gathered for **Activity 1a** in one or two sentences.

_____
_____
_____

Inference

2a Note down three quotations from the extract on page 94 of the Student Book that suggest how Marco feels about the New Society and its rules.

_____
_____
_____

b Write one paragraph answering the question: How does Marco feel about the New Society and its rules? Use some of the quotations you noted in **Activity 2a** in your answer.

_____
_____
_____
_____
_____

Unit 3: A perfect world — Section 1 Exploring a fictional future

Set extension activity

3 You are going to write two diary entries based on the extract on page 94 of the Student Book.

a In the first diary entry, imagine that you are Marco describing a visit to his family on Founders Day. Think about how he feels that he sees them so rarely, how he feels about the New Society, and about whether he is happy with his life. Continue your answer in your notebook if needed.

b In the second diary entry, imagine that you are Marco's sister Anya, describing the same day. Think about how she feels about her brother's status, about his role as a knight, and about the New Society. Continue your answer in your notebook if needed.

Responding to ideas

4a From what you have read in the extract, do you think that life in the New Society is fair? Make some notes using the following prompts.

(i) Things that seem fair.

_____
_____
_____

(ii) Things that seem unfair.

_____
_____
_____

(iii) How the New Society could be fairer.

_____
_____
_____

b Now write a short paragraph answering the question, using your notes and quotations from the extract to support the points you make.

_____
_____
_____
_____
_____

Subjects and verbs

5a Write a cross next to any of the following sentences with incorrect subject–verb agreement.
  (i) Not noticing the unusual silence, he ride his horse through the gate.
  (ii) Behind him, the gate banged shut.
  (iii) He have a sudden thought.
  (iv) This will be going to hurt.
  (v) What would his brother has done?

b Rewrite the incorrect sentences in **Activity 5a**, correcting them as you do so.

_____
_____
_____

Unit 3: A perfect world | **Section 1 Exploring a fictional future** | 89

Set extension activity

6a You are going to plan and write an alternative opening to the extract on page 94 of the Student Book. Your new version should be told from the point of view of the 'tired-looking woman' mentioned in the final paragraph of the original opening. Use your imagination and make some notes using the following prompts.

(i) What is the woman's job?

(ii) Who does she live with?

(iii) How does she and the people she lives with feel about the New Society and its rules?

(iv) How do they feel, and what do they do, when the knight knocks at the door?

b Now write your alternative opening in the space below. Continue your answer in your notebook if needed.

Section 2
Building an argument

In this section, you will practise exploring the structure of an argument text and plan your own.

Identifying key ideas

1 Look again at the article on page 98 of the Student Book. For each paragraph, write a short sentence summarising the key point in your own words.

Paragraph 1 _____

Paragraph 2 _____

_____

Paragraph 3 _____

_____

Paragraph 4 _____

_____

Paragraph 5 _____

_____

Paragraph 6 _____

_____

Exploring structure

2 Look at the three sentences below. Put them in the correct order in the spaces below so that they follow the structure indicated by the questions.
- An unhealthy diet can lead to obesity and other problems.
- We should teach people about nutrition.
- Many people have an unhealthy diet.

a What is the problem?

_____

b Why is it a problem?

_____

c What should we do about it?

_____

Unit 3: A perfect world — Section 2 Building an argument

Set extension activity

3 Complete the tables below, explaining the reasons for these problems and what should be done.

What is the problem? Global temperatures are rising.

Why is it a problem? _____

What should we do about it? _____

What is the problem? The park is too small.

Why is it a problem? _____

What should we do about it? _____

What is the problem? There are lots of potholes in the roads.

Why is it a problem? _____

What should we do about it? _____

What is the problem? My sister cannot swim.

Why is it a problem? _____

What should we do about it? _____

Planning an argument

4 You are going to plan an article for the school newsletter arguing either that schools should insist that pupils wear a school uniform or arguing that school uniforms are a bad idea.

Use the table below to note down your ideas on both sides of the argument.

Schools uniforms are a good idea	Schools uniforms are a bad idea

5 Now select which side you feel most strongly about. Your argument should address a problem. For example, *school uniforms can be expensive*. Note down two or three problems that you could address.

_____

_____

_____

_____

_____

_____

6 Use the table below to plan the structure of your article.

What is the problem?
Why is it a problem?
1 _____
2 _____
3 _____
What should we do about it?

Unit 3: A perfect world
Section 2 Building an argument

Set extension activity

7a Write the article you planned in **Activity 6** in the space below. Remember you are writing to a school newsletter, so your audience is students. Include your most convincing arguments. Continue your answer in your notebook if needed.

b Now write a similar article, making the opposite argument. Continue your answer in your notebook if needed.

Section 3
Choosing vocabulary 1

This section links to pages 102–105 of the Student Book.

In this section, you will practise exploring how writers imply ideas and select vocabulary to add impact to them.

Key points and intentions

1 Look again at the webpage on page 102 of the Student Book.

a What change is the organisation trying to achieve?

_____

b How do they hope to achieve it?

_____

c How do they hope the reader can help?

_____

2 Theirworld's global campaign is aiming to change how the world thinks about early childhood development.

What does this imply about the way the world currently thinks about early childhood development?

_____

3a Look at the sentences below. Which state their point explicitly? Which imply something without stating it explicitly? Write 'stated' or 'implied' next to each sentence.

(i) Cats are very independent. _____

(ii) Cats tend to spend time alone and can hunt birds and mice. _____

(iii) We believe more could be done. _____

(iv) Not enough is being done. _____

b Now look at the following explicit statements. Rewrite them so that the points are implied rather than stated.

(i) Doing exercise makes you feel happy.

_____
_____

(ii) Education is very important.

_____
_____

Unit 3: A perfect world — Section 3 Choosing vocabulary 1

Set extension activity

4 Imagine that the head teacher has decided to rename your school. You have been asked to come up with a new name for the school, along with a new motto. The name and the motto need to imply what is best about the school.

a Note down some ideas about things that are very important for the school to do well.

b Identify the core values that represent the school. For example: *We try to help every student succeed in their studies.* Try to use as few words as possible for each one.

c In the space below, create a name, motto and logo or badge for the school that suggest the values you have identified.

Positive nouns and verbs

5 Read this extract from a letter arguing that an area would benefit from a bigger park.

A new, bigger park at the centre of the community would change everything. My hope is that the council will see the huge long-term benefits of this. A large public space would give the community somewhere to hold events such as fairs and concerts. This would provide opportunities to local businesses as well as helping to bring people together.

Write down at least three positive nouns and three positive verbs from the extract above that help to create a positive tone.

Positive nouns	Positive verbs

6 You are now going to plan to write the next paragraph in the letter. It could focus specifically on the benefits to young people of having a park nearby.

a Note as many positive nouns and verbs as possible that you could use in this new paragraph.

Positive nouns	Positive verbs

b Note down two or three benefits of a new park that you plan to highlight in your paragraph.

c Now write the next paragraph in the letter, using positive nouns and verbs where possible.

d Look back over your paragraph. Are there any opportunities to improve or add to the positive nouns and verbs? Make any relevant changes.

Unit 3: A perfect world — **Section 3 Choosing vocabulary 1**

Set extension activity

7a You are going to write a complete letter to the council arguing for a new local facility of your choice. Examples of a new facility could include a skate park, a community centre, or a swimming pool.

Make some notes using the following prompts.

(i) What problem(s) would the new facility solve?

(ii) What benefits would the new facility offer?

(iii) What positive nouns and verbs can you think of to include in your writing?

b Write your letter in the space below. Continue your answer in your notebook if needed.

Section 4
Choosing vocabulary 2

This section links to pages 106–109 of the Student Book.

In this section, you will practise exploring how nouns and verbs can be modified with adjectives and adverbs to add to their impact.

Understanding the text

1 Look again at the webpage on page 106 of the Student Book.

a How does the writer link the existence of orangutans to the health of the whole planet?

_____

_____

_____

b Why do you think the writer does this?

_____

_____

Commenting on adjectives and adverbs

2 Read the following sentence from the extract on page 106 of the Student Book.

> Orangutans are gentle, intelligent creatures who use their long, powerful arms and dexterous hands and feet to move effortlessly through the rainforest canopy.

Which two adjectives are intended to make the reader feel that orangutans should be respected and protected? Explain your answer below.

_____

_____

3a How are adjectives used to emphasise the seriousness of the problem in this sentence from the extract? Explain your answer below.

> Palm oil is used in over 50 per cent of products on supermarket shelves and is an urgent, ever-growing threat to the future of orangutans.

_____

_____

b Find one other example in the webpage of a sentence in which adjectives or adverbs have been carefully chosen to create a particular response in readers. Write it down and explain its effect.

_____

_____

_____

Unit 3: A perfect world — Section 4 Choosing vocabulary 2

Set extension activity

4 You are going to write a text to persuade people that an endangered species of animal needs protecting. Research and note down all the information you can find about the endangered species of your choice. Use the prompts below to structure your notes.

a What is your chosen animal? Why is it endangered? What needs to change to fix the problem? Continue your answer in your notebook if needed.

_____

_____

_____

_____

_____

_____

_____

_____

_____

b What do you want readers to think and feel?

_____

_____

c What do you want readers to do?

_____

_____

5 Now write your text in the space below. Aim to write at least two paragraphs. Try to choose verbs, adverbs and noun phrases carefully to create the desired response in your readers. Continue your answer in your notebook if needed.

_____

_____

_____

_____

_____

_____

_____

_____

_____

Silent vowels

6 Circle the spelling mistakes in the sentence below.

> I have had a definite intrest in famly history ever since my grandmother, one memorable afternoon, showed me a box of jewelry that she kept seperate from the rest of her things.

b Rewrite the sentence, correcting the mistakes.

_____
_____

Adding impact with noun phrases and adverbs

7 Build noun phrases around each of these words, designed to make them sound like natural wonders.

lake: _____

whale: _____

glacier: _____

cave: _____

8 Add adverbs to the following verbs to make the action sound tense, anxious or rushed.

moved _____

untied _____

said _____

worked _____

9 Look at the following sentence: The bears move through the forest.

(i) Rewrite the sentence, building a noun phrase to make the bears sound magnificent.

_____

(ii) Rewrite the sentence again, building a noun phrase to make the bears sound vulnerable.

_____

(iii) Rewrite the sentence again, this time replacing the verb and adding an adverb to make the bears sound dangerous.

_____

b Write three more sentences about bears, choosing either to make them seem magnificent, vulnerable or dangerous. Use noun phrases and adverbs in your sentences.

_____
_____
_____

Unit 3: A perfect world — Choosing vocabulary 2

Set extension activity

10 Revise the skills you have covered in the first half of this unit, ready for the assessment in the next lesson. You may find it helpful to note down the key points covered in each of the sections so far. If there are any areas where you do not feel confident, reread the appropriate pages in the Student Book.

Section 1: Exploring a fictional future

Understand the key ideas in a text, for example: the characters, the setting and what happens.

Section 2: Building an argument

Section 3: Choosing vocabulary 1

Section 4: Choosing vocabulary 2

Section 5
Assessment

In this section, you will answer questions on a short extract and improve a sample response from a student.

The extract below is a persuasive article about libraries.

▼ Read the article and then answer the questions that follow it.

LIBRARIES ARE IN CRISIS!

Action for Libraries

Campaigning to save local libraries

1 Local libraries across the country are being forced to close in record numbers. The government says that there are more important things to pay for, like hospitals and schools. But libraries have been an important part of local life for over a hundred years. Without local libraries, fewer people of all ages have access to books, fewer people read, and fewer children do well at school. Worse still, the
5 effects are felt mainly by families with less money – wealthier families can afford to buy more books.

That's why Action for Libraries is urging the government to make more funds available to save local libraries from closing.

Libraries matter!
- The National Literacy Trust estimates that children who visit libraries are twice as likely to read well as those who do not.
10 - Report after report shows that young people who read widely are more likely to do well at school and in work. It stands to reason that more people will read widely if they have access to more books.
- Some argue that libraries don't matter anymore because of the invention of eBooks. However, 23 per cent of households do not have a broadband connection so are unable to download eBooks. What's more, evidence shows that words read on a printed page are more likely to be remembered than those read on a screen.
15 - And as celebrated children's writer Michael Edge says, 'Who has ever met a toddler who doesn't like sitting with a friendly adult, turning the pages of a picture book?'

A library isn't simply a warehouse to borrow books from
- A local library is a place to study or read quietly when it is difficult to do so at home for any reason.
- Local libraries often organise talks by visiting writers, helping more people to connect with writers.
20 - Libraries advertise other local arts organisations of all kinds, helping to support local culture.
- local community.
- Libraries are a public place for people to meet, free of charge.

Help us to save our libraries before it's too late!

How you can help
25 - Sign our petition calling for no more libraries to be closed.
- Write to your local politician, arguing to save or reopen your local library.
- Join our peaceful march on 1 January.

Unit 3: A perfect world — **Section 5 Assessment**

Assessment questions

1 What is the problem that this article identifies?

---

2 List three reasons given in the article to explain why the problem matters.

---

3 'Who has ever met a toddler who doesn't like sitting with a friendly adult, turning the pages of a picture book?'

What does this extract from the article imply about the value of eBooks?

---

4 Look at the following question and read the student's response that follows.

Question: How effectively does the writer of the article on page 102 present their argument?

Response: The writer wants people to stop closing librarys because librarys are really impourtant· for people to be able to read books if they cant by them. Young people especially need to read books to help them do well at school and just becuase of ebooks that doesnt mean librarys should close because not everyone has broadband at home. That means closing librarys is bad for everyone but especially people with less money to buy books and have broadband. So the writer really wants everyone to help make the government stop closing librarys.

a What advice would you give to this student to help them improve their resonse?

---

b Write your own improved response to the question in the space below. Continue your answer in your notebook.

Section 6
Supporting key points

In this section, you will practise exploring how writers support their ideas with evidence, examples and explanations.

Evidence

1a Look again at the article on page 112 of the Student Book. In which paragraphs does the writer explain that people appeared to become more intelligent between the 1930s and 1990s?

b What types of evidence does the writer present to support this point?

c What does the evidence tell us?

Points, examples and comments

2 Look at these sentences taken from the article on page 102 of this Workbook 'Action for Libraries).

> 8 • The National Literacy Trust estimates that children who visit libraries are twice as likely to read well as those who do not.
> 10 • Report after report shows that young people who read widely are more likely to do well at school and in work. It stands to reason that more people will read widely if they have access to more books.
> • Some argue that libraries don't matter anymore because of the invention of eBooks. However, 23 per cent of households do not have a broadband connection so are unable to download eBooks. What's more, evidence shows that words read on a printed page are more likely to be remembered than those read on a screen.
> 15 • And as celebrated children's writer Michael Edge says, 'Who has ever met a toddler who doesn't like sitting with a friendly adult, turning the pages of a picture book?'

The overall point of the article is that closing libraries is bad for society because access to printed books is valuable.

a Write down three examples the writer gives that support this central point.

b Write down one comment the writer makes to support this central point.

Unit 3: A perfect world — Section 6 Supporting key points

Set extension activity

3 In a later activity, you will write an article arguing that using a bicycle has a range of benefits.

a Make some notes in the table provided, listing all the possible benefits of bicycles. Include ideas of benefits to the rider as well as benefits to the environment.

Benefits to the rider	Benefits to the environment

b Search online or elsewhere to find evidence that you could use to persuade people of these benefits. You could include statistics, quotes from reports or other articles, examples from your own experience, or direct quotes from experts. If you are unable to search online, make up some suitable facts and statistics. Note down all the evidence you find in the space below.

Sequencing points, examples and comments

4a Look at this short paragraph from the extract on page 102 of this Workbook and complete the table that follows.

> Libraries are in crisis! Local libraries across the country are being forced to close in record numbers. But libraries have been an important part of local life for over a hundred years.

Which sentence states the point?	
Which sentence provides the example or evidence?	
Which sentence contains a comment expressing a point of view?	

b Rewrite the paragraph from **Activity 4a**, putting the sentences in a different order. If necessary, change a few words to make the paragraph make sense.

5 Write your own short paragraph arguing that libraries are important. You could refer back to the article on page 102 of this Workbook (Action for Libraries) to gather some information. Remember to include a point, an example and a comment.

Using fronted adverbials to link sentences

6 Choose suitable adverbials from the list below to fill in the gaps in the sentences that follow.

Furthermore | On the other hand | On the contrary | However

a eBooks can be very convenient. _____ evidence shows that people, especially young children, benefit more from reading printed books.

b Communities in the hottest parts of the world are already struggling with the effects of global warming. _____ the planet as a whole is being damaged by rising temperatures.

Unit 3: A perfect world — Section 6 Supporting key points

Set extension activity

7 Look back at the notes you made for **Activity 3** on page 105 of this Workbook, for an article on the benefits of riding bicycles. You are going to write at least three paragraphs arguing that riding a bicycle is a positive thing to do.

a List at least three main points that you will make. For each one, note down the evidence or example(s) that you will use to support the point.

(i) _____

(ii) _____

(iii) _____

b Now write three paragraphs of your article in the space below. Continue your answer in your notebook if needed. Remember to:
- link your examples and points
- use adverbials to link sentences together where appropriate.

This section links to pages 116–119 of the Student Book.

Section 7
Structuring sentences

In this section, you will practise exploring and experimenting with the impact that different sentence structures can have on your writing.

Evidence

1 Look again at the article on page 116 of the Student Book. Using evidence from the article, complete each of the following points.

a It is important to say thank you _____

_____

b It is not necessary to say thank you _____

_____

Sentence length

2 Rewrite each of these long sentences as two sentences – one longer and one shorter. The shorter sentence should be the one you think should be emphasised.

a We really need your help because the government needs to know that burning fossil fuels is something everyone in the country cares about.

_____

_____

b The ice sheets are melting, the sea levels are rising, species are becoming extinct in record numbers, and time is running out.

_____

_____

c One of the worst things we as individuals can do to the environment is to fly in aeroplanes regularly, so think twice before flying.

_____

_____

3 Write your own point about fighting climate change using two sentences. One should be long and one short. The short sentence should be the one you want to emphasise.

_____

_____

Unit 3: A perfect world
Section 7 Structuring sentences

Set extension activity

4 You are going to practise controlling the length of your sentences.

a Choose a topic or hobby that you are interested in and write ten sentences about it. Each sentence should have more words in it than the sentence before. Consider how long your first sentence should be in order to complete all ten sentences. The sentences do not need to make sense together as one whole passage. Continue your answer in your notebook if needed.

b Now rewrite your sentences in reverse order, so that the last sentence you wrote in **Activity 4a** becomes the first and longest sentence, and the first sentence you wrote becomes the final and shortest sentence. Continue your answer in your notebook if needed.

Using dashes and semi-colons

5a Rewrite this sentence using a semi-colon instead of a conjunction.

I choose not to fly and I prefer the train.

b Rewrite this sentence using a dash instead of a conjunction.

You couldn't outrun a tiger because tigers are much faster than humans.

Experimenting with sentences

6 In each of the following activities you may change a few of the words in the sentences so that your answers make sense. Look at the three sentences below.

- Don't throw plastic in the bin.
- Plastic is bad for the environment.
- Recycle it.

a Rewrite the three sentences as one long sentence using conjunctions.

b Rewrite them again as one long sentence but put the clauses in a different order.

c Rewrite them as two sentences: one should be long and one should be short.

d Choose the version that you think is best, and rewrite it using at least one semi-colon.

Writing sentences

7 You are going to write an article arguing that adults should allow children more freedom. Write one single-clause sentence about each of these topics:

a A situation in which adults should allow children more freedom

b An example showing how adults in this situation could allow children more freedom

c Why adults in this situation should allow children more freedom

Unit 3: A perfect world — Section 7 Structuring sentences

Set extension activity

8 You are going to continue to plan your article arguing that adults should allow children more freedom, which you started in **Activity 7**.

a Make some notes on a further point you could make, using the table below. You need not use only single-clause sentences.

A situation in which adults should allow children more freedom: _____
An example of how adults could do this: _____
The reason adults should do this: _____

b Write your article in two or three paragraphs below and continue writing in your notebook. Remember to use a variety of sentence lengths and structures including, for example:
- shorter sentences for emphasis
- semi-colons, colons or dashes where appropriate
- clauses placed at the end of sentences for emphasis.

Section 8
Using rhetorical devices

In this section, you will practise exploring ways in which rhetorical devices can add impact to your ideas.

Identifying rhetorical devices

1 Read this extract and then answer the questions that follow.

When we go shopping at the supermarket, everything comes wrapped in plastic: fruit in plastic, pasta in plastic, bread in plastic. We all know plastic is bad for the environment. Do the supermarkets really think we would care if they told us to bring our own reusable containers to put our pasta in? If, like me, you want to do something about it, then sign our petition, tell your friends about it, and refuse to buy food wrapped in plastic. Sign it, say it, do it!

a Write down one example of each of the following rhetorical devices from the extract above.

Rhetorical question: _____

Triple structure: _____

List: _____

Direct address: _____

Repetition: _____

b What effect is the paragraph intended to have on the reader?

_____
_____

c Pick four of the examples of rhetorical devices you found in **Activity 1a**. Explain why each one is effective in helping to achieve the intended impact.

- _____
_____
- _____
_____
- _____
_____
- _____
_____

Unit 3: A perfect world — Section 8 Using rhetorical devices

Set extension activity

2 Write ten statements relating to the following idea: we should all use less plastic. Underneath each statement, rewrite it using a rhetorical device. Try to include at least one example of:
- a rhetorical question
- triple structure
- a list
- direct address
- repetition.

Statement 1: _____

Rewritten with rhetorical device: _____

Statement 2: _____

Rewritten with rhetorical device: _____

Statement 3: _____

Rewritten with rhetorical device: _____

Statement 4: _____

Rewritten with rhetorical device: _____

Statement 5: _____

Rewritten with rhetorical device: _____

Statement 6: _____

Rewritten with rhetorical device: _____

Statement 7: _____

Rewritten with rhetorical device: _____

Statement 8: _____

Rewritten with rhetorical device: _____

Statement 9: _____

Rewritten with rhetorical device: _____

Statement 10: _____

Rewritten with rhetorical device: _____

Section 8 Using rhetorical devices

Apostrophes

3 Write 'P' or 'C' next to each of these phrases and sentences to indicate whether it uses an apostrophe of possession or contraction.

a Isn't it strange? _____   **b** Who's going to do more? _____

c Children's happiness is important. _____   **d** China's best kept secret _____

4 Rewrite each of these phrases and sentences using apostrophes where possible.

a It has not yet been proved.
_____

b A parents worst nightmare
_____

c It is not going to work.
_____

d Our schools motto
_____

e Mans best friend
_____

Using rhetorical devices

5 Rewrite these sentences using the rhetorical devices stated.

a People should use less plastic.

Direct address: _____

b We do not want to be surrounded by plastic.

Rhetorical question: _____

c There is plastic in our food, rivers and oceans.

Repetition: _____

d Nearly everything we buy comes wrapped in plastic.

List: _____

e When you find litter, grab it and bin it.

Triple structure: _____

6 Which one of the rewritten sentences from **Activity 5** would make the strongest opening sentence for an article? Explain your answer below.

_____

Unit 3: A perfect world — Section 8 Using rhetorical devices

Set extension activity

7 Look back at the statements you wrote for **Activity 2** on page 113 of this Workbook. You are now going to plan and write an article arguing that we should use less plastic.

a Make some notes below, outlining two paragraphs for the article.

Paragraph 1
Why is the amount of plastic a problem?
Key point/statement: _____
_____
Examples/evidence: _____
_____
_____

Paragraph 2
What should we/the reader do about it?
Key point/statement: _____
_____
Examples/evidence: _____
_____
_____

b Now write your two paragraphs in the space below. Continue your answer in your notebook.

_____
_____
_____
_____
_____
_____
_____
_____

c Look back through what you have written. Are there any opportunities to include more rhetorical devices so that the writing has greater impact? Make any improvements you can.

Section 9
Introductions and conclusions

In this section, you will practise exploring the contribution that introductions and conclusions make to effective argument texts.

Introductions

1 Read this introduction to the article on page 112 of the Student Book and then answer the questions that follow.

> Once upon a time, if I wanted to find my way to somewhere unfamiliar, I would have pulled out a map and plotted my route. These days, I just put the destination into my smartphone and let it make all the decisions. Is this a simple, practical thing to do or, by relying on increasingly smarter phones, are we allowing them to make us, day by day, a little bit dumber?

a Underline the sentence that introduces the topic of the article.

b What is the writer's opinion? _____

c What rhetorical device has the writer used? _____

d How does this rhetorical device help to engage the reader? Explain your answer below.

e What familiar personal example does the writer use in the introduction?

f Explain how the writer's use of a familiar personal example helps to engage the reader.

2a Write an alternative opening sentence to the article that states a surprising fact or opinion directly.

b How effectively does your new opening sentence engage the reader? Explain your answer below.

Unit 3: A perfect world — Section 9 Introductions and conclusions

Set extension activity

3a Look back at the set extension activities in this Workbook in which you have written articles. Select three, and rewrite the opening paragraphs for each one in the tables below, practising the skills you have learnt in this section. Remember that an introduction must:
- introduce the topic
- suggest or state the writer's opinion
- engage the reader.

Effective ways to engage the reader include using an example, perhaps from your own life; a surprising fact or statistic; a dramatic, surprising question; and a rhetorical question.

Introduction 1

Introduction 2

Introduction 3

b Look back over what you have written. Which introduction do you think is the most effective? Explain your answer below.

Section 9 Introductions and conclusions
Unit 3: A perfect world

Conclusions

4 Look at this conclusion taken from the article on page 112 of the Student Book.

> In the years ahead, AI will have an extraordinary impact on our lives, from self-driving cars to robot surgeons, but we would be foolish to allow ourselves to become too reliant on them.

> I like my smartphone. But I like my brain even more.

a Which sentence or phrase summarises the writer's key ideas?

_____

b Which sentence or phrase emphasises the writer's views?

_____

c What does the conclusion make you think and feel? Explain your answer below.

_____
_____

5a Look again at the introductions you wrote for **Activity 3a** on the previous page. Write a short concluding paragraph that would appear at the end of each article. Remember that your conclusion should summarise key ideas and views, and aim to leave the reader thinking about the topic.

Conclusion 1

Conclusion 2

Conclusion 3

b Look back over what you have written. Which conclusion do you think is the most effective? Explain your answer below.

_____

Unit 3: A perfect world — Section 9 Introductions and conclusions

Set extension activity

6 Create a guide to writing an effective persuasive article, using the prompts below.

Introduce the topic here: _____
_____
_____

The introduction should:

- _____
- _____
- _____

Good ways to engage the reader in the introduction include:

- _____
- _____
- _____
- _____

Each paragraph should include:

- _____
- _____
- _____

Using a variety of sentence structures is useful, for example:

- _____
- _____
- _____

The range of rhetorical devices that can be used includes:

- _____
- _____
- _____
- _____
- _____

The conclusion should:

- _____
- _____
- _____

Section 10
Reviewing and revising

In this section, you will practise ways of correcting and developing a response to give it as much impact as possible.

Identifying points, examples and comments

1 Read this example of a student's persuasive article and then answer the questions that follow with a 'Yes' or 'No'.

> We should all grow our own vegetables
>
> When I was growing up, my mother grew her own vegetables in an allotment.
>
> Getting out there, digging, planting and harvesting in the fresh air comes with so many benefits. Doctors recommend that each day we should exercise for 30 minutes, eat five portions of fruit and vegetables, and take every opportunity to spend time outside to boost Vitamin D levels.
>
> Then there are the global benefits to consider. Growing and eating your own vegetables isn't just good for your health, it's good for the health of the planet.
>
> So what are you waiting for? Get your gardening gloves on, get outside and get digging! You'll feel better for it, and you'll be doing your bit to help the planet.

a (i) Does the article have an introduction? _____

(ii) Does the introduction introduce the topic? _____

(iii) Does the introduction introduce the writer's point of view? _____

b (i) Does the second paragraph make a key point? _____

(ii) Does the second paragraph include evidence? _____

(iii) Does the second paragraph explain how the point links to the main argument? _____

c (i) Does the third paragraph make a key point? _____

(ii) Does the third paragraph include evidence or an example? _____

(iii) Does the third paragraph explain how the point links to the main argument? _____

d (i) Does the article have a conclusion? _____

(ii) Does the conclusion summarise the writer's key ideas? _____

(iii) Does the conclusion emphasise the writer's views? _____

2 Based on your responses to **Activities 1a–1d**, what advice would you give to the student on how to improve their article? Write your advice below.

_____

_____

Unit 3: A perfect world — Section 10 Reviewing and revising

Set extension activity

3a Look again at the example student article on page 120 of this Workbook. Rewrite the article, improving it in any way you can.

We should all grow our own vegetables

_____

b How have the changes you made improved the article? Explain your answer below.

_____

Reviewing vocabulary choices and sentence structure

4a Write down five words the student used in their article on page 120 of this Workbook that help to emphasise the positive side of growing your own vegetables.

- _____
- _____
- _____
- _____
- _____

b Identify three opportunities to change or add vocabulary to the student's article, which help emphasise that growing your own vegetables is positive. Write your improved sentences below.

- _____
- _____
- _____

c Identify three different devices in the student's article and write down an example of each.

Device: _____

Example: _____

Device: _____

Example: _____

Device: _____

Example: _____

Checking for careless errors

5 Underline the errors in each of the following sentences and then rewrite them correctly.

a Every morning we would travel to scool by train.

_____

b Plastic is the real problem hear, theirs plastic all over the beach.

_____

c When my my father got home he would always have a storey to tell.

_____

d We simply havent got enogh time to weight for someone else to do something.

_____

e If really want to help you should sign the petition.

_____

Unit 3: A perfect world — Section 10 Reviewing and revising

Set extension activity

6 Revise the skills you have covered in the second half of this unit, ready for the assessment in the next lesson. You may find it helpful to note down the key points covered in each of the sections so far. If there are any areas where you do not feel confident, reread the information given in the Student Book throughout this unit. Think back to when you planned for the previous assessment. What helped? What could you improve on?

Section 6: Supporting key points

Evidence can include an expert's opinion, scientific research and statistics from surveys.

Section 7: Structuring sentences

Section 8: Using rhetorical devices

Section 9: Introductions and conclusions

Section 10: Reviewing and revising

Section 11
Assessment

In this section, you will identify the mistakes in a sample response from a student and write an improved version.

1 Look at the following task and read the student's response that follows.

Task: Write a persuasive article arguing that life would be better if mobile phones did not exist.

Response: If we wont have mobile phones then we could all save monny because their expensive and anyway we didn't really need them because weve got computers and email and we could use landlines for phones. Also because some people have mobiles and some people dont that's not realy fare so we should make it that nobody has them. And mobile phones can be a problem because somtimes people used them to much which can be bad for sleeping and can stop you talking to other people face to face and everybody is always checking their social media and things and getting worried about it.

You are going to improve and extend this response.

a Underline any spelling or punctuation mistakes.
b Underline any verbs that are in the wrong tense.
c Write a 'V' next to any opportunities to improve the impact of the writing by making different vocabulary choices.
d Write an 'S' next to any opportunities to improve the impact of the writing by varying sentence length and structure.
e Write a 'P' wherever you think paragraph breaks should be added.
f Use the space in the box below to make some notes and plan how you will improve this answer.

2 Rewrite your improved version of the response in the space below. Remember to:
- write an engaging introduction
- set out the problems
- explain why they matter
- explain your solution
- use persuasive vocabulary.

Section 1
Summarising

In this section, you will practise your skills in reading, understanding and summarising an information text.

Prefixes and suffixes

1a (i) Underline the prefix in this word: *preschool*   **(ii)** Underline the suffix in this word: *forgiveness*

b Complete the table below, adding five words that use the same prefix that you underlined in **Activity 1a** above, and five words that use the same suffix that you underlined in **Activity 1a** above.

Prefix	Suffix
preview	

Understanding unfamiliar words

2 For each of the following sentences, circle the most likely meaning of the underlined words based on your understanding of the sentence.

a The weather was <u>atrocious</u> and we rushed inside, wet and shivering.

spectacular   impressive   awful   dull   bright

b The question <u>bamboozled</u> him and he stood there, scratching his head.

confused   annoyed   amused   frustrated   inspired

Combining points

3 Look again at the information text on page 136 of the Student Book. Write one or two sentences on what you have learned about the people who played cricket.

_____
_____
_____
_____
_____

Unit 4: World of sport — Section 1 Summarising

Set extension activity

4a Research a sport of your choice and note down everything you can find out about its history in the space below. Include information on how the sport began, who played it, where it was played, what the rules were and how these things changed over time. Continue your answer in your notebook if needed.

b Based on what you have found out, write a short paragraph combining the relevant information to answer the following question: How did the sport change over time?

Writing a summary

▼ Read the extract and then complete the activities that follow.

1 Cricket – The famous grounds of 'Lord's,' and 'The Oval' with the more recently established 'Prince's' are the principal cricket grounds of London. 'Lord's' is the headquarters of the Marylebone Club and, there, some of the 'sensational' cricket of the year is played. Matches between Oxford and Cambridge, and Eton and Harrow – especially the latter – attract society to an almost ridiculous extent, and are among the sights of London. The cricket lover will, however, find many matches more
5 to his taste than these, and as hardly a week goes by in the season from May to September without a first-class match, will have no difficulty in finding a suitable occasion for a visit to the celebrated old place.

'Lord's' is a notoriously difficult ground, but the Marylebone Club has recently expended a great deal of money on improvements. A tavern is attached to the ground and, besides racket and tennis courts, there are billiard-rooms and a variety of grandstands and pavilions. The Marylebone Club (entrance fee, £1; annual subscription, £3) are the present
10 owners of 'Lord's', which is situated on St John's Wood Road.

'The Oval' at Kennington is the headquarters of the Surrey County Cricket Club, and some of the very best matches of the season are played on the ground. A spacious pavilion, a tavern with a billiards room and a large dining room, and racket-courts add to the attractions of 'The Oval'. The ground itself is as near perfection as can be and, in seasonable weather, a wicket can be selected as true as a billiard-table.

5a Note down the key points of information presented in each paragraph of the extract above.

Paragraph 1

Paragraph 2

Paragraph 3

b Using no more than three sentences, summarise the information and ideas in the extract, linking the key information together.

Unit 4: World of sport | **Section 1 Summarising** | 129

Set extension activity

6 Look back through the work you have done in this section and the corresponding section of the Student Book. Write a guide explaining how to summarise a text, using the prompts below.

a Combining points (explain the skill and give an example)

b Summarising a paragraph by using only the key sentence (explain the skill and give an example)

c Summarising all the key information in a paragraph (explain the skill and give an example)

d Now, in as few words as possible, outline your tips on how to summarise an information text.

Section 2
Informing and describing

In this section, you will practise exploring how writers select information and add description to achieve their intention.

Understanding and responding

1 Look again at the extract on page 140 of the Student Book. For each of the following questions, underline the key word or phrase in the question. Then write the answer in the space provided.

a In what sport is Brian Krause champion? _____

b In what year was the free-fall record set? _____

c When was extreme ironing launched? _____

d Which sport involves parents? _____

e Where does worm charming take place? _____

2a For each of the events, note down the piece of information that makes it seem most weird to you.

  (i) Cherry pit-spitting _____

  (ii) World gurning awards _____

  (iii) Worm charming _____

  (iv) Extreme ironing _____

  (v) Baby crawling _____

  (vi) Indoor skydiving _____

b Which sport do you find the least weird? Explain your answer below.

_____
_____
_____

Unit 4: World of sport
Section 2 Informing and describing

Set extension activity

3 Use books or the internet to find out about other weird and wonderful sports. Identify five sports and note down the key information about them. Remember to try and address the questions: **what, when, where, who, how?**

a _____

b _____

c _____

d _____

e _____

Informing and describing

4 For each of the extracts below, write down: one fact the writer presents, one phrase that adds descriptive detail, and one sentence explaining the image or feeling the descriptive detail creates.

a Competitors frame their nastiest expressions through a horse collar and compete for the world championship in Cumbria.

Fact: _____
Descriptive detail: _____
Image or feeling created: _____
_____

b Babies are enticed by their parents – some waving toys – to reach the finish line, crawling in a straight line for five metres.

Fact: _____
Descriptive detail: _____
Image or feeling created: _____
_____

Identifying intentions

5 For each of the short extracts below, write one sentence explaining what the writer's intention is. For example, *The writer's intention is to make us feel sympathy for the character when she describes him 'shivering and crying'.*

a She gave us a steely stare, then turned on her heel. That's when we saw the 'I'm a fluffy unicorn' sticker on her back.
_____
_____

b The forest was now completely dark. My neck prickled at every rustle. Then I heard a grunt, and the sound of a branch being torn from a tree. I froze.
_____
_____

c Anish sat slumped against a wall, all the fight knocked out of him. I called over to him and it was all he could do to turn his tear-stained face in my direction.
_____
_____

d Take care near the edge. The water is freezing at this time of year. If you fall in you will be dead in under a minute.
_____
_____

e At last it had arrived! Mei tore open the letter, her eyes sparkling.
_____

Set extension activity

6a Look back at the information you researched and noted down about weird sports for **Activity 3** on page 131 of this Workbook. Choose three of them and write a paragraph for each one, providing the relevant information and using descriptive details to make them sound as weird and entertaining as possible.

(i) _____

(ii) _____

(iii) _____

b Read back over what you have written. Which sport sounds the weirdest based on your descriptions? Explain your answer below.

Section 3
Selecting evidence

This section links to pages 144–147 of the Student Book.

In this section, you will practise your skills in selecting relevant, focused evidence to support your response to an information text.

Finding and inferring information

1 Look again at the article extract on page 144 of the Student Book and then answer these questions.

a How does the writer imply that sepak takraw is more difficult than volleyball?

b What material is the sepak takraw ball made from?

c How does the writer imply that sepak takraw was not originally a competitive sport?

d Which paragraph explains the rules of the modern game?

e Note down all the information given in that paragraph.

Vocabulary choices

2 Look at the following extracts and then answer the questions.

a It may be difficult to imagine a sport which combines elements of volleyball, badminton and football.

Which word or phrase suggests that sepak takraw is an unusual sport?

b with players demonstrating breathtaking agility and strength: leaping, twisting and kicking to get the ball past their opponents.

Which word or phrase suggests that skill levels are very high?

Unit 4: World of sport Section 3 Selecting evidence

Set extension activity

3 Read through the article extract on page 144 of the Student Book again and note down seven words or phrases that you feel have been carefully chosen to create a particular effect. For each one, write a sentence explaining the effect the writer has created.

a Word or phrase: _____

Response: _____

b Word or phrase: _____

Response: _____

c Word or phrase: _____

Response: _____

d Word or phrase: _____

Response: _____

e Word or phrase: _____

Response: _____

f Word or phrase: _____

Response: _____

g Word or phrase: _____

Response: _____

Clauses

4a How many clauses are there in each of these sentences from the article on page 144 of the Student Book?

(i) The name is a combination of words from two languages;

(ii) In 1933, a net was introduced, and in the following 20 years, the competitive version of the game spread rapidly across Southeast Asia, and formal rules were introduced.

(iii) Chinlone is considered to be a graceful, non-competitive sport.

(iv) The beautiful movements are also one of the main attractions in sepak takraw.

b Rewrite sentence (ii) above as three single-clause sentences.

Using evidence

5 Look at the following point made by a student, which uses evidence from the article extract to support their answer:

> The writer implies that the sport requires players to be very fit and skilful: 'The sport is similar to volleyball, however, whereas in volleyball the players keep the ball aloft with their hands, sepak takraw players must use the feet, chest, knees or head — a rule which requires amazing athleticism.

a Which word or phrase from the quotation that the student uses best supports the point they make?

b Rewrite the point, using only the word or phrase as the evidence, rather than the whole sentence.

6a Reread the article extract on page 144 of the Student Book and note down a sentence that could be used as evidence to support the point that the writer presents chinlone players as impressive to watch.

b Now choose the shortest possible part of the sentence to use as evidence. Write a sentence, using evidence, to make the following point: The writer presents chinlone players as impressive to watch.

Unit 4: World of sport
Section 3 Selecting evidence

Set extension activity

7 You are going to write a response to the following question: How does the writer present chinlone and sepak takraw as slightly different?

a Note down any key differences the writer mentions about chinlone.

_____
_____
_____
_____

b Note down any significant words or phrases the writer uses to create an impression of how chinlone differs from sepak takraw.

_____
_____
_____
_____

c Write one or two paragraphs responding to the question: How does the writer present chinlone and sepak takraw as slightly different? Remember to use short quotations as evidence.

_____
_____
_____
_____
_____
_____
_____
_____
_____
_____
_____

d Look back over what you have written. If you were marking your response, what advice would you give yourself about how to improve it?

_____
_____

Section 4
Exploring vocabulary choice

In this section, you will practise exploring the writer's choice of vocabulary.

Identifying key information

1 Look again at the article on page 148 of the Student Book.

a Who is the fierljeppen world record holder? _____

b What does the word *fierljeppen* mean in English? _____

c How many Dutch fierljeppers are there? _____

d In which countries has the sport appeared on TV? _____

Intention and vocabulary

2 Look again at paragraph 1 of the article, which introduces the sport of fierljeppen.

a In only **one** word or phrase, describe the impression that the writer has created of fierljeppen in this paragraph.
_____

b Note down **all** of the words or phrases in paragraph 1 that help to create the impression you noted.
_____

3 Find and write down quotations that support each of the following statements.

a People of all ages take part in fierljeppen.
_____

b Large crowds watch the championships.
_____

c Fierljeppen used to be seen as a bit strange.
_____

d More and more people watch the events on TV.
_____

Unit 4: World of sport
Section 4 Exploring vocabulary choice

Set extension activity

4 You are going to rewrite the first two paragraphs of the article on page 148 of the Student Book twice, choosing different vocabulary to give different impressions of the sport.

a Note down all the words and phrases that make the sport seem exciting or dangerous.

b Rewrite the paragraphs, choosing vocabulary that makes the sport sound boring. You may want to change the words and phrases you selected for **Activity 4a**. Continue your answer in your notebook if needed.

c Rewrite the paragraphs, choosing vocabulary that makes the sport sound funny. You may want to change the words and phrases you selected for **Activity 4a**. Continue your answer in your notebook if needed.

Register

5a Look at the following sentences. Three are in a formal register and two are in an informal register. Write F (formal) or I (informal) next to each one.

(i) It's really sunny, there's no wind and it's going to be an awesome day. _____

(ii) Yesterday, the team trained with sumo wrestlers to work on their power. _____

(iii) The crowd gasped when he dropped the ball. _____

(iv) She was so cool after the race, doing selfies and autographs and all that sort of thing. _____

(v) It takes years of work to become world champion. _____

b Now rewrite the two sentences that you marked as 'informal' in a formal register.

(i) _____

(ii) _____

Choosing evidence

6a Note down the individual words or phrases that suggest there is a less serious side to the sport.

_____

b Explain how the vocabulary the writer has chosen indicates the less serious side of the sport. Make sure you mention specific vocabulary choices.

_____
_____

Connotations

7a Complete the table below with each word's connotations. An example is provided.

Word	Connotations
sprints	fast, racing
lurches	
explosion	

Word	Connotations
stunning	
passionate	
oddity	

b Find the word *lurches* in the article. At this point in the article, what impression is the writer intending to give of the sport?

_____
_____

c Write a sentence describing how the writer's use of *lurches* contributes to their intention.

_____
_____

Unit 4: World of sport
Section 4 Exploring vocabulary choice
141

Set extension activity

8 You are going to write a response to the following question: What impression do the writer's vocabulary choices create of the way people feel when they watch fierljeppen?

a Reread the article on page 148 of the Student Book and note down each sentence that relates to the way people feel when they watch fierljeppen. Continue your answer in your notebook if needed.

b Note down any powerful vocabulary you can find in the sentences you have selected.

c Write your response to the question in the space below, remembering to focus on vocabulary choices and their impact. Continue your answer in your notebook if needed.

Section 5
Writing a response

In this section, you will practise your skills in responding to a text.

Gathering information and responding to the text

1a Look again at the newspaper article on page 152 of the Student Book. Note down two key facts presented about each of the three sports.

(i) Bobsleigh: _____

_____

(ii) Skeleton: _____

_____

(iii) Luge: _____

_____

b Which sport seems the least dangerous? Explain your answer below.

_____

_____

Evidence of intention

2a Note one quotation from the article that makes bobsleigh sound like a unique experience.

_____

b The writer says of skeleton that 'of all the Olympic sports, this has to be the scariest'. What information does the writer give to persuade us of this? Use a quotation in your answer.

_____

_____

c Rewrite the following sentence from the extract, using vivid descriptions to make it sound more exciting.

> The brakeman's job only begins at the end of the course when he releases steel spikes into the ice to stop the bob.

_____

_____

d Which words or phrases from your answer to **Activity 2c** above best create a sense of excitement?

_____

Unit 4: World of sport — **Section 5 Writing a response**

Set extension activity

3 Using books or the internet, search for a description of a dangerous extreme sport. Use the information you find to complete the activities below.

a What information about the sport has the writer presented?

b What is dangerous about this sport?

c What words and phrases has the writer used to create a sense of danger or excitement?

d Write one or two paragraphs explaining how the writer has created a sense of danger or excitement. Continue your answer in your notebook if needed.

Sentence starts

4a For each of these sentences, copy out the main clause, the subordinating conjunction and the subordinate clause.

(i) Skeleton is the most frightening because your face is so close to the ice.

Main clause: _____

Subordinating conjunction: _____

Subordinate clause: _____

(ii) The bobsleigh has brakes although they cannot be used until the end of the run.

Main clause: _____

Subordinating conjunction: _____

Subordinate clause: _____

b Now rewrite each of the sentences from **Activity 4a**, reordering them to begin with the subordinating conjunction and subordinate clause.

(i) _____

(ii) _____

Writing paragraphs

5 You are going to plan a paragraph in response to the following question: What impression of bobsleigh do we get from the facts that the writer presents?

a Note down all the facts that the writer presents about bobsleigh on page 152 of the Student Book.

_____

_____

_____

_____

b What impression of bobsleigh does this information help to create?

_____

_____

c Write your paragraph in the space below. Remember to make at least one key point, use quotations from the article as evidence, and comment on the effect of the writer's language.

_____

_____

_____

_____

Set extension activity

6 Revise the skills you have covered in the first half of this unit, ready for the assessment in the next lesson. You may find it helpful to note down the key points covered in each of the sections so far. If there are any areas where you do not feel confident, reread the appropriate pages in the Student Book.

Section 1: Summarising

Decode unfamiliar words by identifying common prefixes and suffixes.

Section 2: Informing and describing

Section 3: Selecting evidence

Section 4: Exploring vocabulary choice

Section 5: Writing a response

Section 6
Assessment

In this section, you will answer questions on a short extract and improve a sample response from a student.

The extract below is taken from a non-fiction text about the sport of yabusame.

▼ Read the extract and then answer the questions that follow it.

1   Imagine standing rooted to the spot as a samurai warrior gallops on horseback towards you, two lethal swords at his waist. As his horse thunders down the hill you see that he is not holding the reins. Instead he holds a long bow, bent fully back. With a cry, he releases an arrow so long it resembles a spear. It spits through the air and buries itself deep in a target.

    This is the sport of yabusame, and it is as close as you will ever get to meeting a traditional samurai warrior. Yabusame, or
5   mounted archery, has very simple rules. The rider may shoot three arrows as they ride at full speed past a row of targets. Points are awarded for the number of targets hit. It is very unusual for a rider to hit three targets in one ride.

    Yabusame requires the participant to have extraordinary skill both as a rider and an archer. He must control the horse using only his legs, and must hit a target while moving at a full gallop.

    The sport is many centuries old and is still practised today, in part as a way to preserve traditional Japanese values of
10 discipline and honour. The rules of the sport, as well as the equipment used by competitors and the way they dress, have not changed since the twelfth century. And despite the fact that yabusame competitors must commit to an extended and intensive training regime, they receive no money from the sport, instead competing simply for the honour of taking part.

Assessment questions

1 What weapons does a yabusame competitor carry in addition to his bow and arrows?

2 Which paragraph explains the rules of yabusame?

3 What two things must the competitor do that require great skill?

4 Look at the opening sentence. What words or phrases has the writer used to make the experience of watching yabusame seem frightening?

5 How does practising yabusame link to traditional Japanese values?

Unit 4: World of sport — **Section 6 Assessment**

6 Summarise the key points of the extract in no more than 50 words.

7 Look at the following task and read the student's response that follows.

> **Task:** Explain the impression the writer has created of yabusame.
>
> **Response:** Yabusame is very exciting and dangerous because the riders have weapons and they shoot arrows while they are riding. It's a bit like watching a real samurai warrior because they dress the same and they have swords and they get points for hitting targets which is what they used to do a long time ago. I think it would be quite frightening to watch yabusame because of the weapons and the riders can't hold the reins of the horses because they have to shoot the arrows. It is Japanese and hundreds of years old and the rules are quite simple. You do it for honour not money.

a What advice would you give to the student to help them improve their response?

b Write your own improved response to the task in the space below.

Section 7
Structuring an information text

This section links to pages 158–161 of the Student Book.

In this section, you will practise exploring ways of structuring information texts to guide the reader and convey information effectively.

Reading and understanding

1 Look again at the extract on page 158 of the Student Book.

a What modern game does *Harpastum* and *Episkyros* most resemble? _____

b Where was Kemari played? _____

c Why was football banned at times during its early history?
_____

d When were the rules of Association Football agreed? _____

Intention

2 Reread the first paragraph of the extract. What detail is used to grab the reader's interest?
_____

3a Look at the fourth paragraph of the extract which begins *Football became …* Complete the following sentences.

(i) The main purpose of this paragraph is to _____
_____

(ii) The writer intends to make the topic more interesting by mentioning _____
_____

(iii) These details _____ the reader.

b Which paragraph do you find the most interesting? Explain your answer below.
_____
_____
_____

Unit 4: World of sport — Section 7 Structuring an information text

Set extension activity

4 Research the history of a sport you find interesting that has not been covered in previous sections. Note down everything you can find out about it using the following headings as prompts.

a How and where did the sport begin?

b How did the sport develop over time?

c How is it played today?

d What kind of people played it in the past?

e Are there any interesting heroes, traditions or other surprising facts about the sport?

Paragraph structure

5 Look again at the first paragraph of the extract on page 158 of the Student Book.

a What is the key point of this paragraph?

_____

b What examples or details are used to support the key point?

_____

_____

Presenting an information text

6 When a paragraph or section of text contains a list of facts or points that are equally important, these are sometimes presented using bullet points.

a Which paragraph in the extract on page 158 of the Student Book contains a list of points that are equally important?

_____

b Rewrite the paragraph as a list of bullet points.

_____

_____

_____

_____

_____

_____

_____

c Write a short paragraph arguing that this paragraph would be better presented using bullet points, explaining your reasons.

_____

_____

_____

_____

7 Look back at **Activity 4** on page 149 of this Workbook. Soon you will be asked to write this information as an information text. Begin planning by identifying three or more short subheadings that you could use to divide the information into sections. Write the subheadings below, along with a one-sentence summary of what kind of information each section will include.

_____

_____

_____

Unit 4: World of sport — Section 7 Structuring an information text

Set extension activity

8 Look back at the information you gathered for **Activity 4** on page 149 of this Workbook. You are going to write an information text about your chosen sport, using the information. Remember to:
- divide your text into sections with short subheadings
- consider using bullet points where sections contain a list of equally important points
- ensure, where possible, that sections or paragraphs have a key point supported by interesting or informative examples and details
- consider including a fact box to give more information about a particular topic.

Write your text in the space below. Continue your answer in your notebook if needed.

Section 8
Exploring vocabulary and sentence choices

In this section, you will practise exploring the writer's choice of different sentence structures and their impact on the reader.

Responding to vocabulary choices

1 Look again at the article on page 162 of the Student Book.

a Reread the first paragraph. What impression does the noun phrase 'rusted iron roofs' create?

_____
_____

b Identify one other word or phrase in the paragraph that creates a similar impression.

_____

c Which phrase in the second paragraph suggests that cricket is central to village life?

_____

d Reread the third paragraph, which begins *Former national captain…* Which one word in this paragraph tells us how cricketers are viewed?

_____

e Reread the fourth paragraph, which begins *The cars, too…* What does the verb describing the cars, 'creeping', suggest about attitudes to cricket?

_____
_____

2a How does the writer create the impression that people are willing to make great efforts to be involved in cricket? Explain your answer below, using short quotations from the article.

_____
_____
_____
_____

b How does the writer create the impression that this village is central to the sport of cricket throughout Papua New Guinea? Explain your answer below, using short quotations from the extract.

_____
_____
_____

Unit 4: World of sport — Section 8 Exploring vocabulary

Set extension activity

3 Go back through the article on page 162 of the Student Book. Identify any words or short phrases that the writer has used to help create a particular impression. For each one, write a short sentence explaining the impression that the word or phrase creates.

Word or phrase	Impression created

Single-clause and multi-clause sentences

4a Rewrite the sentence from the article below as two single-clause sentences.

> Down by the water, the houses are built on stilts and reach a hundred metres out into the ocean.

b Rewrite the two sentences from the article below as one multi-clause sentence, linking them with a conjunction.

> Cricket is a way of life here. The kids love it.

c Rewrite the sentence from the article below as two single-clause sentences.

> These new cricket stars are not the product of an English village green or a sunbaked sporting ground in Australia, but a single coastal village with a pitch on the main street.

Sentence structure

5 Look at these two versions of the same sentence.
- 'I LOVE CRICKET!' read the simple message scrawled in red paint on a sheet that hung from the balcony.
- Scrawled in red paint on a sheet that hung from the balcony, the simple message read, 'I LOVE CRICKET!'

a Which version of the sentence has the greatest impact? Explain your answer below.

b Complete the following sentence: Writers often place the words they want to emphasise at the _____ of a sentence.

6 Look at the following pair of sentences and the different orders in which they are presented.
- Cricket is not just a game or a hobby here in Papua New Guinea. It's a way of life.
- Cricket is a way of life here in Papua New Guinea. It's not just a game or a hobby.

a Which version of the sentences has the greatest impact? Explain your answer below.

b Based on your answers to **Activities 5 and 6a**, write a sentence explaining how writers use sentence structure to emphasise certain points.

Unit 4: World of sport Section 8 Exploring vocabulary

Set extension activity

7 You are going to write a response to the following question: The writer suggests that to many people in Papua New Guinea, cricket is the most important thing in their life. How has the writer created this impression?

a Look again at the article on page 162 of the Student Book. Plan your response using the following prompts.

(i) What information suggests that cricket is very important to people?

_____
_____
_____
_____

(ii) What particular words or phrases in the extract convey this impression most strongly?

_____
_____
_____
_____

(iii) What information suggests that people play the game with great enthusiasm?

_____
_____
_____
_____

(iv) What particular words or phrases in the extract convey this impression most strongly?

_____
_____
_____
_____

b Write your response in the space below. Continue your answer in your notebook if needed.

_____
_____
_____
_____
_____
_____

Section 9
Planning a critical response

In this section, you will practise your skills in identifying significant choices the writer has made, so that you can comment on their effect.

Structure

▼ Reread the extract from page 146 and then answer the questions that follow it.

> 1   Imagine standing rooted to the spot as a samurai warrior gallops on horseback towards you, two lethal swords at his waist. As his horse thunders down the hill you see that he is not holding the reins. Instead he holds a long bow, bent fully back. With a cry, he releases an arrow so long it resembles a spear. It spits through the air and buries itself deep in a target.
>
> This is the sport of yabusame, and it is as close as you will ever get to meeting a traditional samurai warrior. Yabusame, or
> 5   mounted archery, has very simple rules. The rider may shoot three arrows as they ride at full speed past a row of targets. Points are awarded for the number of targets hit. It is very unusual for a rider to hit three targets in one ride.
>
> Yabusame requires the participant to have extraordinary skill both as a rider and archer. He must control the horse using only his legs, and must hit a target while moving at a full gallop.
>
> The sport is many centuries old and is still practised today, in part as a way to preserve traditional Japanese values of
> 10   discipline and honour. The rules of the sport, as well as the equipment used by competitors and the way they dress, have not changed since the twelfth century. And despite the fact that yabusame competitors must commit to an extended and intensive training regime, they receive no money from the sport. They compete for the honour of taking part.

1a Summarise each paragraph in one short sentence.

Paragraph 1: _____

Paragraph 2: _____

Paragraph 3: _____

Paragraph 4: _____

b Why do you think the writer has put the paragraphs in this order? Explain your answer below.

_____
_____
_____
_____
_____

Unit 4: World of sport
Section 9 Planning a critical response

Set extension activity

2 Look back through the texts you have read in the Student Book so far. Select three texts and, for each one, answer the following question: How has the structure of the text helped the writer to achieve their intention?

Text 1: _____

Text 2: _____

Text 3: _____

Vocabulary

3 Identify two words or phrases from different parts of the extract on page 156 of this Workbook that help create a vivid image in your mind. For each one, write a sentence with the quotation embedded, explaining the image that it creates.

a _____

_____

b _____

_____

4 Identify two words or phrases from different parts of the extract that show the writer is trying to create a powerful response in the reader. For each one, write a sentence with the quotation embedded, explaining the response that it creates.

a _____

_____

b _____

_____

Sentence structure

5 Identify two parts of the extract where the writer uses sentence structure to emphasise something important. For each one, write a sentence with the quotation embedded, explaining how the writer has used sentence structure for effect.

a _____

_____

b _____

_____

Planning

6 What are the benefits of using a list when gathering your points and planning a response? What are the benefits of using a spidergram? Note your ideas in the table below.

Benefits of a list	Benefits of a spidergram

Unit 4: World of sport — Section 9 Planning a critical response — 159

Set extension activity

7 You are going to write a one-page guide to planning a critical response.

a Look back through pages 166–169 of the Student Book and write a short summary of how to plan a response. Try to include advice on:
- how to gather ideas
- what to comment on
- how to structure points.

Summary: _____

b Now provide an example plan for a response to the extract about yabusame on page 156 of this Workbook.

Section 10
Comparing information texts

This section links to pages 170–173 of the Student Book.

In this section, you will practise comparing the information in two extracts and the writers' different intentions.

Comparing key information

1 Reread Extract B on page 171 of the Student Book, as well as the article extract about sepak takraw on page 144 of the Student Book, and then answer the following questions.

Complete the following table to help you compare the two texts.

	Extract B	Sepak takraw
What information is provided on the history of the sport?		
What detail is provided on the rules of the sport?		
What examples are there of vivid description of the sport?		

2 Using the notes you made in **Activity 1**, answer the following questions.

a Which text includes the most information about the history of the sport? _____

b Which text describes the rules in most detail? _____

c Which text gives the most vivid description of the sport? _____

d Based on what you have read, what are the similarities between volleyball and sepak takraw?
_____
_____
_____
_____

| Unit 4: World of sport | Section 10 Comparing information texts |

Set extension activity

3 You are going to write a short comparison of two sports of your choice. Aim to choose sports that have something in common: for example, two extreme sports or two team ball games.

a Make some notes briefly covering the following:

(i) Rules of the sport

Sport 1: _____

_____

_____

Sport 2: _____

_____

_____

(ii) The experience of playing or watching the sport

Sport 1: _____

_____

_____

Sport 2: _____

_____

_____

b Now write two paragraphs comparing the sports, identifying similarities and differences between them. Use adverbials of comparison in your answer.

_____

_____

_____

_____

_____

_____

_____

_____

_____

_____

_____

_____

Comparing intention

4 Find at least one quotation from each text ('Sepak takraw' from page 144 of the Student Book and 'Extract B: Volleyball' from page 171 of the Student Book) to support the following statements.

a The writer intends to help readers understand the rules of the sport.

Sepak takraw: _____

Volleyball: _____

b The writer intends to emphasise the skill and athleticism of the participants.

Sepak takraw: _____

Volleyball: _____

c The writer intends to make the sport sound exciting.

Sepak takraw: _____

Volleyball: _____

5 You are going to plan a response comparing the two texts.

a Note down key similarities and differences between the types of information provided in each text.

_____

_____

_____

b Note down key similarities and differences between the intentions of the writers.

_____

_____

_____

c Write your response comparing the two texts below. Write one paragraph comparing the kind of information presented, and a second paragraph on the writers' intentions. Remember to use short quotations from the texts to support the points you make. Continue your answer in your notebook if needed.

_____

_____

_____

_____

_____

_____

_____

_____

Unit 4: World of sport — Section 10 Comparing information texts

Set extension activity

6 Revise the skills you have covered in the second half of this unit, ready for the assessment in the next lesson. You may find it helpful to note down the key points covered in each of the sections so far. If there are any areas where you do not feel confident, reread the information given in the Student Book throughout this unit. Think back to when you planned for the previous assessment. What helped? What could you improve on?

Section 7: Structuring an information text

Consider your personal response to a text. For example, what did you find interesting?

Section 8: Exploring vocabulary and sentence choices

Section 9: Planning a critical response

Section 10: Comparing information texts

Section 11
Assessment

In this section, you will identify the mistakes in a sample response from a student and write an improved version.

The extract below is an information text about the sport of water polo.

▼ Read the extract and then answer the questions that follow it.

Sink or swim

1 Water polo is not for the fainthearted! The rules are simple enough. There is a goal similar to a small football goal at each end of the 30-metre pool. Seven players on each team compete to score goals by passing to each other and throwing a ball past a goalkeeper and into the opposition goal. Outfield players can only hold the ball with one hand, although the goalkeeper can use both.

5 A game lasts for 32 minutes, which may not sound like long until you learn that at no point is a player allowed to touch the floor or sides of the pool. What's more, the game is played at a truly breathless pace. Teams have a mere 30 seconds to score once they have the ball. After that, the ball is handed over to the other team, and so on.

In order to take a more powerful shot, a player will kick so that their upper body rises out of the water, giving them a height advantage and freeing their arms and torso from the water to throw. A professional player can kick up so high that their
10 whole body, from the waist up, is out of the water – without kicking off the floor. This, of course, uses up huge amounts of energy.

Players swim around two miles per game without rest, requiring extraordinary levels of fitness. And it's not just an endurance event, it's more of a sprint – or hundreds of sprints. Players stop, tread water, change direction, sprint forwards, backwards, grapple for the ball, dive, kick, leap, throw, and repeat over and over again. No wonder many describe water
15 polo as the most intense and exhausting Olympic sport!

1 Look at the following question and read the student's response that follows.

Question: What impression does the writer create of water polo?

Response: Water polo is in a swimming pool and its a bit like football because there is too goals and you had to score by getting the ball into the goal and theirs a goalkeeper. There was 32 minutes in a game which is quite short compared to football and some other sports and theirs some different rules like you only have 30 seconds to score and then you've got to give the ball to the other team and then they have a go at scoring. To take a shot you have to kick up out of the pool to get higher up which is hard and it makes it easier to shoot. Its really tiring because players had to swim about two miles in a game.

You are going to improve and extend this response.

a Underline any spelling or punctuation mistakes.

b Underline any verbs that are in the wrong tense.

Unit 4: World of sport — Section 11 Assessment

c Write a 'V' next to any opportunities to improve the impact of the writing by making different vocabulary choices.

d Write an 'S' next to any opportunities to improve the impact of the writing by varying sentence length and structure.

e Use the box below to make some notes and plan how you will improve and extend this answer.

2 Rewrite your improved version of the answer in the space below. Continue your answer in your notebook. Remember to:

- address what impression is created
- address how the impression is created
- use quotations from the extract to back up points made
- write at least three paragraphs.

Section 1
Writing autobiographically

In this section, you will practise exploring some of the key features that help writers to explain and describe a moment in time.

Identifying key ideas

1 Look again at the extract on page 178 of the Student Book. Look at paragraphs 3 to 5, from 'I remember another beach party' to 'I can't feel my body'. Note down all the information that you learn or infer from this part of the extract.

_____
_____
_____
_____

Pulling ideas together

2 In two separate and very different memories, the writer uses an identical description of one part of his mother's appearance. Write down the repeated description and explain its effect.

_____
_____
_____

3a Look through the whole extract and note down how the narrator remembers feeling at each stage.

_____
_____
_____
_____

b Write a paragraph answering the following question: How do the writer's emotions change throughout this extract?

_____
_____
_____
_____
_____

Unit 5: A moment in time | **Section 1 Writing autobiographically**

Set extension activity

4a Rewrite the extract from page 178 of the Student Book as a chronological account in the past tense. The first sentence has been given as an example. Continue your answer in your notebook if needed.

On my fifth birthday, we went to the beach.

b Which version, the original or your rewritten version, do you think has the greatest impact on the reader? Explain your answer below.

Summarising

5 Look again at the extract on page 178 of the Student Book. Write a short summary of the second paragraph, including how old the writer is at this point, how he feels and what is happening.

_____
_____
_____

Responding to ideas

6a Although he is describing memories, the writer uses the present tense in his descriptions. Note down three examples of sentences written in the present tense that you found particularly powerful.

_____
_____
_____
_____
_____

b How does the use of the present tense help to engage the reader? Explain your answer below.

_____
_____
_____
_____
_____

7a Note down three examples from the extract where the writer describes memories linked to physical sensations.

_____
_____
_____
_____
_____

b How does the writer use information about his physical sensations to engage the reader? Write a paragraph explaining your answer below.

_____
_____
_____
_____
_____

Unit 5: A moment in time — Section 1 Writing autobiographically

Set extension activity

8 You are going to write one-paragraph descriptions of memories linked to the prompts below. For each one, try to combine facts, senses, emotions and (where relevant) dialogue.

a A memory of something unpleasant

b A very happy memory from early childhood

c A memory about your family

d A memory about your first days at school

Section 2
Exploring structure and intention

This section links to pages 182–185 of the Student Book.

In this section, you will practise exploring how writers structure a text to control the reader's response.

Inferring ideas

1 Look again at the article on page 182 of the Student Book. For each of the quotations below, write a sentence explaining what the writer feels, or wants the reader to feel, at this point.

a blood was oozing out on the deck

_____
_____

b Peering anxiously over the side of the boat, we saw grey-black shadows circling in the blue.

_____
_____

c their movement in the water graceful and smooth

_____
_____

d I dared myself to reach up and touch one, gingerly reaching out

_____
_____

2a Write down at least three feelings about sharks that the writer suggests the divers experienced before, during or after the dive.

_____

b Write a short paragraph describing the different impressions of the sharks created by the writer as the article progresses. Use quotations from the article to support your observations.

_____
_____
_____

Unit 5: A moment in time | Section 2 Exploring structure and intention | 171

Set extension activity

3 You are going to gather different (real or fictional) ideas for a piece of writing in which you encounter something that you first have negative feelings about, and then find that your feelings become more positive as the encounter progresses. Use the prompts to complete the tables below.

You meet a stranger
What are your negative feelings?
What about the encounter changes your feelings?
How do you feel by the end of the encounter?

You encounter a creature
What are your negative feelings?
What about the encounter changes your feelings?
How do you feel by the end of the encounter?

You take part in an activity you have never wanted to try
What are your negative feelings?
What about the experience changes your feelings?
How do you feel by the end of the experience?

First, second and third person

4 Look again at the fourth paragraph of the extract and rewrite it in the third person. The first sentence has been given as an example.

Meanwhile, the divemaster signalled to them to mingle with the sharks.

Creating a response

5a How does the writer create feelings of tension and fear in the extract?

(i) Write down two or three quotations that you can use in your answer.

(ii) Write one paragraph, using the quotations you have selected to support the points you make.

b How does the writer present the sharks in a positive light?

(i) Write down two or three quotations that you can use in your answer.

(ii) Write one paragraph, using quotations from the article to support the points you make.

Unit 5: A moment in time — Section 2 Exploring structure and intention

Set extension activity

6 Look back at **Activity 3** on page 171 of this Workbook. You are now going to choose one of the scenarios and write a text in which you describe an encounter or experience. You should describe initial feelings of fear turning to more positive feelings by the end of the scene.

a Make some notes using the following prompts. Make sure you expand on any notes you made for **Activity 3**.

(i) What or who do you encounter?

_____

_____

(ii) What negative feelings do you want to suggest in the first part of the text? What phrases or vocabulary could you use to convey those feelings?

_____

_____

_____

_____

(iii) What positive feelings do you want to suggest by the end of the text? What phrases or vocabulary could you use to convey those feelings?

_____

_____

_____

_____

b Write your text in the space below. Continue your answer in your notebook if needed.

_____

_____

_____

_____

_____

_____

_____

_____

_____

Section 3
Using narrative structure

In this section, you will practise exploring ways in which you can engage readers by structuring your text like a story.

Key information

1 Look again at the article on page 186 of the Student Book.

a What caused Zhifa to gasp in shock? _____

b Why were Zhifa and his brothers digging? _____

c How did the brothers hope to benefit from their discovery?
_____

d Who was Qin She Huang? _____

Narrative structure

2 Think of a story you know well. It could be a fairy tale, other story or film plot. Complete the table below to outline its narrative structure.

Title:
Exposition: What is the problem?
Conflict: What obstacles are faced trying to deal with the problem?
Climax: What is the final confrontation between the character(s) and the problem?
Resolution: How is the problem resolved?

Unit 5: A moment in time | **Section 3 Using narrative structure**

Set extension activity

3 You are going to plan an article about a group of students making a surprising accidental discovery at your school. Come up with a list of events leading to the discovery and resulting from the discovery. Use the questions below to structure your ideas.

a What are the students doing that leads to the discovery?

b Why are they doing this? What problem are they facing?

c How does the problem get worse before it gets resolved?

d What do they discover and how does this happen?

e How does the discovery help them resolve their problem?

f Are there any other interesting or amusing details or events that you might include in the story?

Writer's intention

4 Look again at the article on page 186 of the Student Book.

a Circle or underline two of the following words that you feel best describe the writer's intention.

    engage   amuse   inform   persuade

b For each intention you have identified, find two quotations from the article that support it.

(i) _____

_____

(ii) _____

_____

c Write two short paragraphs, one for each of the intentions you have identified. In each paragraph, explain why you believe this is the writer's intention. Use quotations from the article to support the points you make.

(i) _____

_____

_____

_____

(ii) _____

_____

_____

_____

Chronological or non-chronological structure

5 Think of a story you know well: for example, a fairy tale.

a Write down the key events of the story in chronological order.

_____

_____

_____

_____

_____

_____

b Which event would you begin the story with if you wished to engage the reader with a surprising or mysterious opening? Explain your answer below.

_____

_____

_____

Unit 5: A moment in time — Section 3 Using narrative structure

Set extension activity

6 Look back at the plan you began in **Activity 3** on page 175 of this Workbook. You are going to write the article about a surprising accidental discovery at your school.

a Make some notes below, indicating the order in which you will describe events. Try to begin with a surprising or mysterious event to engage the reader.

b Write your article in the space below. Continue your answer in your notebook if needed.

This section links to pages 190–193 of the Student Book.

Section 4
Choosing precise vocabulary

In this section, you will practise exploring the importance of careful vocabulary choice when you are writing to explain and to describe.

Responding to vocabulary choice

1 Look again at the article on page 190 of the Student Book. For each paragraph of the text from paragraph 5 to paragraph 12, choose one powerful word or phrase that the writer has chosen and comment on the effect of it. Paragraph 4 has already been completed as an example.

Paragraph 4 _Describing the arrival of the sharks, the writer says, 'suddenly, they were upon us'._
This gives the impression of fast-paced action, and a sense of being overwhelmed.

a Paragraph 5 _____
_____

b Paragraph 6 _____
_____

c Paragraph 7 _____
_____

d Paragraph 8 _____
_____

e Paragraph 9 _____
_____

f Paragraph 10 _____
_____

g Paragraph 11 _____
_____

h Paragraph 12 _____
_____

Unit 5: A moment in time — Section 4 Choosing precise vocabulary

Set extension activity

2 You are going to plan an article describing a day that you remember really enjoying. Make some notes using the questions below as prompts.

a Write a brief overview describing what sort of day it was. What were you doing?

_____

_____

b What powerful words or phrases could you use to convey the impression the day made on you?

_____

_____

c What is your single fondest memory of the day?

_____

_____

d What powerful words or phrases could you use to convey the impression that it made on you?

_____

_____

e What else happened that day to make it so memorable?

_____

_____

f What powerful words or phrases could you use to describe these events?

_____

_____

3 Now write your article in the space below. Continue your answer in your notebook if needed.

_____

_____

_____

_____

_____

_____

_____

_____

Using a thesaurus

4 Look at the sentence below. In this sentence, the word *keen* should be replaced with something more powerful to really convey the sense of not being able to 'contain my excitement'.

It looked like such fun and I could barely contain my excitement — I was so keen to have a go.

Some synonyms of 'keen' that you would find in a thesaurus include:

| eager | animated | ebullient | desperate | breathless |

a Write down the dictionary definitions of each of these words that most closely link to the meaning of the word *keen*.

eager: _____

animated: _____

ebullient: _____

desperate: _____

breathless: _____

b Choose the word that you think works best and copy out the sentence above, replacing the word *keen* with your choice.

_____

_____

Choosing vocabulary

5 Rewrite each of these sentences, replacing the underlined words with more powerful alternatives.

a When I saw her stepping off the train, I <u>ran</u> towards her.

_____

b I was <u>nervous</u> that she wouldn't recognise me.

_____

c I had grown a lot and when she saw me, she looked <u>surprised.</u>

_____

d But I could tell at once that she was <u>happy</u> to see me.

_____

e I really can't describe how <u>nice</u> it was to see her again.

_____

f The <u>sadness</u> of the last three years melted away.

_____

Unit 5: A moment in time — Section 4 Choosing precise vocabulary

Set extension activity

6 Revise the skills you have covered in the first half of this unit, ready for the assessment in the next lesson. You may find it helpful to note down the key points covered in each of the sections so far. If there are any areas where you do not feel confident, reread the appropriate pages in the Student Book.

Section 1: Writing autobiographically

Identify the key ideas in a text to check your understanding.

___

Section 2: Exploring structure and intention

___

Section 3: Using narrative structure

___

Section 4: Choosing precise vocabulary

___

Section 5
Assessment

This section links to pages 194–195 of the Student Book.

In this section, you will answer questions on a short extract and improve a sample response from a student.

The extract below is taken from a memoir about learning to ride a bike.

▼ Read the extract and then answer the questions that follow it.

Just like riding a bike

1 I remember that wall rushing towards me as if it were yesterday. I truly don't think I've experienced total panic quite like that ever since.

Mum and Dad held to the sink-or-swim view of parenting. We never had stair gates and I can remember to this day howling with shock and rage as a toddler, wedged at the bottom of the stairs I had just fallen down at home. Mum set me on my feet
5 again, kissed my head, and suggested I take care on the stairs.

When they thought I was ready to read a book without pictures, they handed me a copy of *Gulliver's Travels,* an eighteenth-century story about adventure and meeting new people from new lands. Somehow I clawed my way to the end, barely understanding, but understanding something all the same (rather like the hero of the story).

And when they thought I was ready to ride a bike, they put me on a bike and gave me a push. I wobbled my way along the
10 road outside our house and collapsed into the kerb, a shrieking heap of metal and torn skin.

Try again, Mum told me. So I did. Little by little my body and brain grew accustomed to the shape and feel of the thing, and soon enough I was able to pedal in a straight line without injuring myself. Or so I thought.

Our road ended at a pub car park. There was no gate or kerb separating the road from the car park, the one thing just merged into the other. I set off down the road towards the car park, determined to find out how fast I could make the bike
15 go. At first I was delighted with the results, whizzing past the allotments on my right and feeling for the first time the cyclist's breezy rush of freedom.

It was only as I hurtled into the car park that I realised I didn't know how to stop. I looked ahead. The wall of the pub raced to meet me. I braced myself and gripped the handlebars in terror. Then, with a horrible crunch, everything went black.

Assessment questions

1 Does the writer use a chronological or non-chronological structure?

_____

2 Look at the opening paragraph. Why do you think the writer chose to begin his story in this way?

_____
_____
_____

Unit 5: A moment in time — **Section 5 Assessment** — 183

3 What three examples does the writer give of his parents' 'sink or swim' approach to parenting?

4 Write down three examples of vocabulary choices the writer has made that help him to convey the sense of excitement he felt when he set off towards the car park.

5 Look at the final paragraph. How have the writer's vocabulary choices helped to create a sense of his fear?

6 Look at the following question and read the student's response that follows.

Question: How effectively has the writer engaged the reader in this text?

Response: Its about the writer growing up and how his parents weren't very good because they didn't have stair gates and they use to let him fall down the stairs and then they made him read boring books but it sounds like his Mum loved him. One time when he was learning to ride a bike he found it quite difficult and then when he tried to go faster he ended up crashing into a wall because he doesn't no how to use the brakes yet.

a What advice would you give to the student about how to improve their answer?

b Write your own response to the task in the space below. Aim to write at least two paragraphs. Continue your answer in your notebook if needed.

Section 6
Expressing feelings

In this section, you will practise exploring different ways in which writers convey thoughts and feelings.

Inferring ideas

1a Look again at the second paragraph of the text *Just like riding a bike* on page 182 of this Workbook. Why might the writer's mother have decided not to use stair gates to prevent her child from falling down the stairs? Explain your answer below.

b Look at the third paragraph. Which word implies that the writer found the book difficult to read? Explain your answer below.

c Look at the fourth paragraph. How did the writer feel when he fell off his bike? Explain your answer below, using at least one quotation from the text.

Responding to people

2a Note down everything that you learn about the writer's mother. What does she do or decide, and what does this suggest about her personality?

b How do you think the writer wants the reader to respond to his depiction of his mother? Explain your answer below.

Unit 5: A moment in time — Section 6 Expressing feelings

Set extension activity

3 Look at the sentences below. Rewrite each sentence twice in different ways, but each time taking care to imply the emotion in the sentence rather than stating it. An example is provided.

He was very angry.

He punched the door so hard that a crack appeared in one of the panels.

His eyes blazed and he stamped his foot.

a She was delighted.

b I was very nervous.

c They were excited.

d She was terrified.

e He was irritated.

f They were pleased with themselves.

g I felt really relaxed.

h She was curious.

i He was bored.

Direct and reported speech

4 Rewrite the following sentences, punctuating them correctly.

a Come here, she ordered.

b 'I'm busy at the moment' I told him.

c She reassured him that 'she would not be late.'

5 Rewrite the following sentences using direct speech.

a She complained that the water was cold.

b He insisted that he was innocent.

c My sister told me that I couldn't borrow her jumper.

Planning an account

6 You are going to plan an account of a (real or fictional) time when you did or went to something you had been looking forward to for a long time, such as a birthday party. Focus your account on how you felt before and during the event. Use the table below to plan the structure of your account.

Exposition	Where were you? Who was there? Use details to describe the scene.
Conflict	Were you worried about anything?
Climax	What happened at the event? Did anything go wrong? What was the highlight?
Resolution	How did the event end? How did your feelings change?

Unit 5: A moment in time — Section 6 Expressing feelings

Set extension activity

7 Continue with the plan you began in **Activity 6** on the previous page.

a Make some notes below, listing ways that you could imply rather than state the emotions you felt.

b Write your account in the space below. Continue your answer in your notebook if needed.

c Look back over your account. Are there any opportunities to improve the structure of your account of how you have inferred the emotions you felt? Make any relevant changes.

Section 7
Structuring paragraphs

In this section, you will practise exploring the structure of paragraphs when writing to explain and describe.

Exploring structure

1 Look again at the extract on page 200 of the Student Book. What key points, evidence or other information are contained in each paragraph? Summarise them below.

Paragraph 1

Key point: _____

Evidence/other information: _____
_____

Paragraph 2

Key point: _____

Evidence/other information: _____
_____

Paragraph 3

Key point: _____

Evidence/other information: _____
_____

Paragraph 4

Key point: _____

Evidence/other information: _____
_____

2 The writer could have chosen to place the fourth paragraph after the first paragraph. Reread the extract in that order: Paragraph 1 ⟶ Paragraph 4 ⟶ Paragraph 2 ⟶ Paragraph 3

Which order do you prefer? Explain your answer below.

_____
_____
_____
_____

Unit 5: A moment in time — **Section 7 Structuring paragraphs**

Set extension activity

3 You are going to research information to help you write an article explaining the Northern Lights or Aurora Borealis.

a Note down what you find out that explains what the Northern Lights are, as well as how, when, where and why they occur. Continue your answer in your notebook if needed.

___

b Look back over what you have noted. Write three key points that could be the topic sentences of three paragraphs in an article describing and explaining the Northern Lights.

(i) _____

(ii) _____

(iii) _____

Paragraph breaks

4 Look again at the extract about the Tunguska event on page 200 of the Student Book. Explain why the writer began each new paragraph when they did. An example is provided.

Paragraph 2: *The second paragraph contains a change of setting as the focus moves from ground-level Siberia to a global view of the event.*

Paragraph 3: _____

Paragraph 4: _____

Paragraph planning

5 Look back at the notes you made on the Northern Lights for **Activity 3** on page 189 of this Workbook. Use them to plan three paragraphs for your article on the subject. Identify the key point in each paragraph and then add at least two pieces of supporting information per paragraph.

Paragraph 1
Key point: _____

Supporting information: _____

Paragraph 2
Key point: _____

Supporting information: _____

Paragraph 3
Key point: _____

Supporting information: _____

Unit 5: A moment in time — Section 7 Structuring paragraphs

Set extension activity

6 Write your article describing and explaining the Northern Lights in the space below. Aim to write three paragraphs on this topic. Remember to make sure that each paragraph contains a key point as well as supporting information.

Section 8
Experimenting with sentences

In this section, you will practise exploring different ways in which sentences can be structured to add clarity and impact to a writer's ideas.

Identifying intention

1a Look again at the article on page 204 of the Student Book. What is a lightbulb moment?

b What common misconception is the writer trying to correct in this article?

c Why do you think the writer used the invention of the lightbulb as the example to demonstrate the lengthy process of invention? Explain your answer below.

Sentence structure

2 Reread the final paragraph of the article.

> Finally, the lightbulb was cheap enough and efficient enough to be used in homes, shops and factories – but it was the work of many scientists over many years. It was most certainly **not** the result of a lightbulb moment!

a How do you think the writer decided which sentence should be long and which should be short?

b The writer could have chosen to structure the final paragraph like this:

The lightbulb was most certainly not the result of a quick lightbulb moment or flash of inspiration by one genius inventor. It took years to develop.

What is the key difference between the two versions?

c Why might it have made more sense to use the second version from **Activity 2b**?

Unit 5: A moment in time — Section 8 Experimenting with sentences

Set extension activity

3 Practise combining longer sentences with shorter sentences for emphasis. For each of the topics below, write a two-sentence paragraph including a short sentence for impact and a longer descriptive sentence. Try to vary the order so that in some instances you place the short sentence at the beginning, and in others at the end. An example is provided.

Pizza

Whether you like vegetables, meat, cheese, hot and spicy flavours or sweet and fruity flavours, this greatest of Italian inventions has it covered. Pizza is the supreme king of food.

a Your favourite animal

b A theme park

c The most boring thing you have ever done

d Home

e School

f The weather

g Family

h Your future

i Your favourite television programme

Restructuring sentences

4 Look at the following pairs or groups of single-clause sentences. Rewrite each group as one multi-clause sentence, using subordinating conjunctions that indicate time.

a I jumped out of bed. I brushed my teeth.

_____

b I ate some breakfast. I stared out of the window.

_____

c I grabbed my bag. I said goodbye to Mum. I rushed out of the front door.

_____
_____

5 Now rewrite your multi-clause sentences, placing the clauses in a different order without changing the meaning.

a _____

b _____

c _____
_____

Structuring sentences for clarity

6 Look at the following five points.
- I was sitting in my bedroom.
- I was worried about my friend, who had seemed unhappy all day.
- I really wanted to cheer her up.
- I heard my brother playing music in his room.
- I knew what I had to do – I would organise a party for my friend.

a Rewrite these points as a paragraph with no more than three sentences.

_____
_____
_____
_____

b Now rewrite the points as two long sentences.

_____
_____
_____

c Which version do you prefer? Explain your answer below.

_____
_____

Unit 5: A moment in time — **Section 8 Experimenting with sentences**

Set extension activity

7 You are going to plan and write an account of a time when you had to practise hard to learn how to do something: for example, learning to ride a bike or play an instrument. It could be a real or made-up account.

a Write a list of six or seven key points. Aim to set the scene, describe your actions, describe any failed attempts, describe finally succeeding, and describe how you feel at different stages in the process.

b Now write your account, using a mixture of single-clause and multi-clause sentences.

c Rewrite your account, varying the sentence structures you have used so that you break some multi-clause sentences in single-clause sentences, and combine some single-clause sentences into multi-clause sentences.

d Now choose your favourite combinations from each version, and write a final version below.

Section 9
Experimenting with openings

In this section, you will practise exploring ways to engage your reader with an effective opening.

Exploring openings

1a Look at these openings from texts you have encountered already in this unit, and for each one, explain how the opening engages the reader.

> The morning of the shark dive, we were on the boat. It was a beautiful day and I wondered if I wouldn't be happier sunning myself on deck. Captain 'Snoopy' Cooper, our dreadlocked captain, turned the boat in circles, the engines revving furiously as a sign for the sharks to roll up for dinner. The noise and smoke added to the tension, and the adrenaline was pumping quickly.

(i) Response: _____

_____

_____

> Yang Zhifa leapt back as he emptied his bucket of soil onto the ground. A lump, almost a sphere rolled briefly along the dry, stony ground. A head – a human head! Even as Zhifa gasped in shock, he realised there was something strange about it.

(ii) Response: _____

_____

_____

> I remember that wall rushing towards me as if it were yesterday. I truly don't think I've experienced total panic quite like that ever since.

(iii) Response: _____

_____

_____

b Which opening do you find the least engaging? Explain your answer below.

_____

_____

_____

c Rewrite the opening you found the least engaging in a way that you think might better engage the reader.

_____

_____

_____

_____

Unit 5: A moment in time — Section 9 Experimenting with openings

Set extension activity

2 Create a worksheet to help students understand how openings are used to engage readers. Use the prompts below to structure your worksheet.

a What do writers try to achieve in their openings?

b How do writers do this?

c Find and copy out an opening to a text that you find particularly engaging.

d Rewrite the opening so that it is much less engaging.

e Explain why the first version of the opening is more engaging.

Adverbials of time

3 Read the following summary of a student's account of overcoming their fear of speaking in public.
- I was asked to deliver a speech to the whole school during assembly.
- I decided to try and overcome my fear and agreed to make a speech.
- I wrote the speech.
- I practised the speech the day before.
- I had nightmares about it going wrong.
- I arrived at school and hid.
- The head teacher found me and walked me to the school hall.
- I stood up in front of everyone.
- The hall was silent.
- I began to speak.
- I realised people were interested and that they were listening.
- I wasn't afraid any more.

Write these points up as a one-paragraph summary, using adverbials of time to guide the reader where appropriate.

_____
_____
_____
_____
_____
_____

Selecting an opening

4 Choose three different points from the summary above that could provide an engaging way of opening the account. For each one, write the opening sentence. Then explain why you think this would be a good way to start the account.

Point 1: _____

Opening sentence: _____

Explanation: _____

Point 2: _____

Opening sentence: _____

Explanation: _____

Point 3: _____

Opening sentence: _____

Explanation: _____

Unit 5: A moment in time — Section 9 Experimenting with openings

Set extension activity

5a Look back at the three possible openings you began in **Activity 4**. Extend each one to write a full opening paragraph that engages the reader.

Opening 1: _____

Opening 2: _____

Opening 3: _____

b Which opening do you think is most effective? Explain your answer below.

Section 10
Experimenting with endings

In this section, you will experiment with creating a satisfying ending for your writing.

1 Reread the following summary of a student's account of overcoming their fear of speaking in public.
- I was asked to deliver a speech to the whole school during assembly.
- I decided to try and overcome my fear and agreed to make a speech.
- I wrote the speech.
- I practised the speech the day before.
- I had nightmares about it going wrong.
- I arrived at school and hid.
- The head teacher found me and walked me to the school hall.
- I stood up in front of everyone.
- The hall was silent.
- I began to speak.
- I realised people were interested and that they were listening.
- I wasn't afraid any more.

a Write three sentences, explaining three emotions that the student might be feeling as the story unfolds.

_____
_____
_____
_____
_____

b The story is about a student overcoming a fear. What feelings should they experience at the end of the story? Write a sentence or two explaining your answer.

_____
_____
_____

c Note down three possible scenarios in which you could show the student experiencing those feelings at the end: for example, with their friends after the assembly.

_____
_____
_____

Unit 5: A moment in time — Section 10 Experimenting with endings

Set extension activity

2a Look back at the three possible scenarios you suggested in **Activity 1c**. Extend each one to write a full final paragraph that concludes the story by showing that the student has overcome their fear, and conveying the emotions that they feel.

Ending 1:

Ending 2:

Ending 3:

b Which ending do you think is most effective? Explain your answer below.

Beginning, middle and end

3 You are going to plan an account of a time when something went terribly wrong, but the problem was overcome and everything ended well. It could be real or made up.

a Make some notes using the prompts below.

(i) What is the setting? What are you trying to do? How do you feel?

___

___

___

(ii) What happens to start with? How do you feel?

___

___

___

(iii) What goes wrong? How do you feel?

___

___

___

(iv) How do you overcome the problem? How do you feel?

___

___

___

b Select the best opening moment for your story that will engage the reader, and write a short opening paragraph.

___

___

___

___

___

c Think about the emotions you want to convey at the end of the story, when things are resolved, and write a short final paragraph.

___

___

___

___

Set extension activity

4 Revise the skills you have covered in the second half of this unit, ready for the assessment in the next lesson. You may find it helpful to note down the key points covered in each of the sections so far. If there are any areas where you do not feel confident, reread the information given in the Student Book throughout this unit. Think back to when you planned for the previous assessment. What helped? What could you improve on?

Section 6: Expressing feelings

Description can be used in a text to imply something rather than directly stating it.

Section 7: Structuring paragraphs

Section 8: Experimenting with sentences

Section 9: Experimenting with openings

Section 10: Experimenting with endings

Section 11
Assessment

In this section, you will identify the mistakes in a sample response from a student and write an improved version.

1 Look at the following task and read the student's response that follows.

Task: Describe a time when you achieved something you were not sure you were capable of. Your achievement could be real or imagined.

Response: I am going to describe how I learned to stand up on a surf bored. Its really difficult because its really wobbly in the water and you keep falling off especially because there are waves all the time. The first time I tryed it I thought it will be easy but it isnt. I keep falling over and sometimes it hurt quite a lot because you can bang into the surf board. And one of the difficult things is getting the surfboard threw all the waves that have already broken and their pushing you back towards the beach. Anyway youve got to get threw all the broken waves and then ly on top of the surf board and waite for a good wave to come along and then youve got to point the bored towards the beach and start paddling and kicking and then when the wave gets to you youve got to try and stand up at just the rite time when the wave started pushing you so if you got the timing wrong you miss the wave and then youve got to start all over again. In the end I did it but only after lots of falling off.

You are going to improve and extend this response.

   a Underline any spelling or punctuation mistakes.
   b Underline any verbs that are in the wrong tense.
   c Write a 'V' next to any opportunities to improve the impact of the writing by making different vocabulary choices.
   d Write an 'S' next to any opportunities to improve the impact of the writing by varying sentence length and structure.
   e Write a 'P' wherever you think paragraph breaks should be added.
   f Use the space in the box below to make some notes and plan how you will improve this answer.

2 Rewrite your improved version of the answer in the space below. Remember to
- choose an engaging opening
- use the four-part narrative structure
- use a variety of sentence lengths
- use paragraphs
- choose a satisfying ending.

Section 1
Curtain up

This section links to pages 220–223 of the Student Book.

In this section, you will practise exploring ways in which a play can engage its audience.

Reading between the lines

1a Look again at the extract on page 220 of the Student Book. Read the line below from the extract and explain what it suggests about the reason Terry climbed the pylon.

> Perhaps you ain't our mate, then. Perhaps you don't like us at all. That means you're the kind of person who'd sneak on us.

_____

_____

b Complete the following sentence: Sammy warns Terry not to climb the pylon but Sammy is not willing _____

c Look at the final stage direction in the extract, which begins with *Terry starts to climb...* What does this stage direction suggest about Pete?

_____

_____

2a What can you infer from the extract about the relationship between Stubbs and Pete?

_____

_____

_____

_____

b One student said: 'All of the characters are responsible for Terry climbing the pylon.' Do you agree? Explain your answer below.

_____

_____

_____

_____

c Who do you think is most responsible for Terry feeling that he has to climb the pylon? Explain your answer below.

_____

_____

_____

Unit 6: Dramatic! — Section 1 Curtain up

Set extension activity

3 You have been asked to write a short paragraph describing each of the characters and the setting of the extract on page 220 of the Student Book for a group of students who are about to begin rehearsing a performance. Use all the information you can infer from the extract and use your imagination to describe appearance and personalities.

Terry

Sammy

Stubbs

Pete

Kathy

The setting

Beginnings

4 Look again at the points in the plot of the play *The Terrible Fate of Humpty Dumpty*. Write an opening line of dialogue for each point, as if it is the first line of the play. Remember to state who is speaking and try to convey a powerful emotion.

a Terry starts a new school.

_____
_____

b Terry is bullied.

_____
_____

c Terry's only friend, Sammy, will not stand up for him.

_____
_____

d Terry is electrocuted.

_____
_____

e Sammy tells the police what happened.

_____
_____

5 Choose the story point from **Activity 4** that you think would make the most effective alternative opening scene for the play and plan how the scene will unfold using the prompts below.

a Which characters are involved and what do they do?

_____
_____
_____

b What do you want to show the audience about the characters?

_____
_____
_____

c What emotions do you want to convey?

_____
_____

Set extension activity

6 Write the scene that you planned in **Activity 5**. Continue your answer in your notebook if needed. Remember to think about:

- how the character's words reveal things about them and the other characters
- how stage directions can add physical actions to the dialogue and outline the setting
- how to present the script using the conventions of playscripts.

Section 2
Setting the scene

This section links to pages 224–227 of the Student Book.

In this section, you will practise exploring how a writer can introduce setting, mood and character in just a few lines at the very beginning of a playscript.

Building a picture

1 Look again at the opening stage directions from the extract on page 224 of the Student Book.

> *(Desks in rows fill the stage, facing out towards the audience. Students in uniform are sitting on their desks or standing around, talking. There is sudden silence from all students except Liam. They slide slowly into their seats, looking forwards. They respond as though a teacher in front of them is calling out their names to check attendance. Liam remains sitting on Darren's desk, chatting.)*

a Note down all the information that is stated or implied about characters and setting in these stage directions.

_____
_____
_____
_____

b Based only on these stage directions, what do we learn about Liam's character?

_____
_____

Creating mood and character

2a Look again at the extract on page 224 of the Student Book. Find and write down a line of dialogue that reveals something about Liam's character. Write one sentence explaining what reveals.

_____
_____

b A student wrote: 'The writer is trying to create a mood of joy in this opening'. Explain why you agree or disagree with this statement in the space below.

_____
_____
_____
_____
_____

Unit 6: Dramatic! — Section 2 Setting the scene

Set extension activity

3 You are going to rewrite the extract on page 224 of the Student Book, changing the mood to one of extreme tension and anxiety.

a Make some notes using the following prompts.

(i) What might the characters be anxious about?

_____
_____
_____

(ii) How might the different mood change what the characters do and say?

_____
_____
_____

b Rewrite the scene in the space below. Continue your answer in your notebook if needed.

_____
_____
_____
_____
_____
_____
_____
_____
_____
_____
_____
_____
_____
_____
_____
_____

Drama terminology

4 Write definitions for each of these drama terms. If you are not sure, look them up in a dictionary.

Audience: _____

Character: _____

Dialogue: _____

Playwright: _____

Rehearse: _____

Rehearsal: _____

Scene: _____

Scenery: _____

Stage directions: _____

Theatre: _____

Exploring the playwright's intentions

5a Complete the sentence below using one of the word options that follow.

The playwright intends to create a scene that is very _____ to the audience.

strange | familiar | uncomfortable | surprising

b Explain your choice in the space below.

_____
_____
_____

Writing a scene

6 You are going to plan your own scene of a play. It should feature a small group of characters on a school trip to a museum. You could include a teacher and/or museum guide, or just focus on a small group of students. Note down ideas for three to five characters, giving each a short description of names, ages and personalities. Continue your answer in your notebook if needed.

_____
_____
_____
_____
_____
_____
_____

Set extension activity

7a Continue planning the scene you started in **Activity 6**. Make some notes outlining how what the characters say could let the audience know:

- where they are
- what they are doing
- what the mood of the scene is
- aspects of their personalities.

b Write your scene in the space below. Continue your answer in your notebook if needed.

Section 3
From page to stage

This section links to pages 228–231 of the Student Book.

In this section, you will practise exploring ways in which a script can be created from a story written in prose.

Key information

1 Look again at the extracts from the playscript and from the novel on pages 228 and 229 of the Student Book. You have been asked to write some notes on the extracts for actors who will perform the play, giving as much physical description of the characters and setting as possible. Write your notes in the space below, based on the information in the extract from the novel that is not conveyed in the script.

_____
_____
_____
_____
_____
_____

Inferring key information

2 Find a quotation from the playscript that suggests each of the following:

a The man is hungry. _____

b Pip is scared of the man. _____

c The man has escaped from prison. _____

Explaining differences between the extracts

3a Why has the scriptwriter not included much physical description of the characters and setting in the play extract? Explain your answer below.

_____
_____
_____

b In the novel, the man places Pip on a tombstone after emptying his pockets. Why does the scriptwriter not include this point of action? Explain your answer below.

_____
_____
_____

Unit 6: Dramatic!
Section 3 From page to stage

Set extension activity

4 Look again through the playscript below. After each line of dialogue, write a stage direction suggesting how the character should move or speak. It may help to refer back to the extract from the novel on page 229 of the Student Book. An example is provided for you.

(A graveyard)

Pip   *(Reading the names on a grave)* Philip Pirrip … Georgiana, his wife … and their five sons, Alexander, Bartholomew, Abraham, Tobias, and Roger …

(Pip looks sad as he slowly reads out the names. He touches the grave with one hand. A man in wet, muddy clothes jumps out. He has a chain around his leg. He grabs Pip by the chin.)

Man   Keep still or I'll cut your throat.

Pip   Please don't cut my throat, sir. Please!

Man   Tell me your name! Quick!

Pip   It's Pip, sir.

Man   Louder!

Pip   Pip, sir.

Man   Show me where you live. Point out the place!

(Pip points. The man turns Pip upside down. A piece of bread falls out of his pocket. The man eats it greedily.)

Man   What fat cheeks you've got. I feel like I could eat them, and I might!

Pip   Please! No!

Man   Where's your mother?

Pip   There, sir! (Points at the grave.) Georgiana. That's my mother.

Man   Oh, and is that your father too, buried there?

Pip   Yes sir. My father too – also dead.

Comparing the script and the novel

5a Explain the impression you get of the way Pip feels about the man in the playscript.

_____

_____

b Is your impression exactly the same or slightly different when you read the novel extract? Explain your answer below.

_____

_____

c Explain the impression you get of the way the man feels about Pip in the playscript.

_____

_____

d Is your impression exactly the same or slightly different when you read the novel extract? Explain your answer below.

_____

_____

e Which version – the playscript or the novel – gives the strongest sense that Pip is in real danger? Explain your answer below.

_____

_____

f How would you advise the actor playing the part of the man to speak and move to make the character seem as threatening as possible?

_____

_____

_____

g How would you advise the actor playing the part of the man to speak and move to make the character seem less of a threat to Pip?

_____

_____

_____

Unit 6: Dramatic!
Section 3 From page to stage

Set extension activity

6 You are going to rewrite a passage from a fiction text as a playscript. Choose a passage from a fiction text that you have enjoyed. Try to ensure the passage describes a dramatic moment involving two characters in conflict.

a Note down all the information that your playscript will need to convey in order to give the right impression of the characters and their relationship.

b Indicate which elements in your notes from **Activity 6a** can be delivered through dialogue, and which will be described through stage directions covering physical movement, setting and costume.

c Write your script in the space below. Continue your answer in your notebook if needed.

Section 4
Creating conflict

This section links to pages 232–235 of the Student Book.

In this section, you will practise exploring how playwrights can use conflict to shape stories.

Creating conflict

1a Look again at the extract on page 232 of the Student Book. Why might the brother and sister both feel angry towards their father for forcing them to decide between possessions and a blessing?

_____

_____

b Why might the brother feel angry towards his sister?

_____

_____

c Why might the sister feel angry towards her brother?

_____

_____

d Describe the conflict between the brother and the neighbours.

_____

_____

_____

2 Look again at this line of dialogue.

> **Brother** All right then, to show you I'm not completely heartless, to prove that I'm a fair-minded man and to shut up the lot of you — I allow my sister to keep this fine cooking pot. There! She's entitled to nothing and I've given her the pot. Now leave me alone!

a What does the dialogue reveal about how the brother feels towards the neighbours? Support your answer with a quotation.

_____

_____

_____

b What does the dialogue reveal about how the brother feels towards his sister? Support your answer with a quotation.

_____

_____

Unit 6: Dramatic! Section 4 Creating conflict

Set extension activity

3 Look at the examples of conflict below. For each one, try to think of a story you know that includes this kind of conflict. It could be from a book, a film or anything else. Describe how the conflict appears and how it is resolved in the story. If you cannot think of an example, try to make up your own.

a Two characters want the same thing, but only one can have it.

_____
_____
_____
_____

b A character faces a difficult choice, where what they want is different to what they think is right.

_____
_____
_____
_____

c Two characters want very different things.

_____
_____
_____
_____

d A character is in conflict with nature.

_____
_____
_____

e A character is trapped.

_____
_____
_____
_____

f A character has to choose between two things that they want.

_____
_____
_____

Building a story

4 Write down the basic plot of a well-known story, for example a fairy tale, which concludes with the selfish characters being punished and the selfless characters being rewarded for their actions.

_____
_____
_____
_____
_____
_____

5 Write an outline for your own play about two characters who face a choice, in which one makes a selfish choice and the other makes a selfless choice. Use the prompts below to structure your plan.

a Who are the two characters (including their characteristics)?

_____
_____

b What choice do they face?

_____
_____

c What does each character choose?

_____
_____

d How do they feel about one another after the choice?

_____
_____

e How do their choices lead to conflict between them?

_____
_____
_____

f How do other characters help intensify the conflict?

_____
_____

g How is justice done by the end of the story?

_____
_____

Set extension activity

6 Using the notes you made for **Activity 5**, write a scene for your play in which there is obvious conflict between the characters.

This section links to pages 236–239 of the Student Book.

Section 5
Crafting characters

In this section, you will practise exploring how playwrights use dialogue to create character.

Exploring character through language

1 Look again at the extract on page 236 of the Student Book.

a What do you imagine that Flora is thinking during the conversation?

b What do you imagine that Flora is trying to achieve in this scene?

c How does the way that Flora speaks give you this impression?

d What impressions do you get of Flora's character? For example, is she kind or rude?

e Write down two or three short quotations from the extract that give you these impressions.

2a In your own words, summarise the conflict between Max and Flora expressed in the extract.

b Which character does the playwright want the audience to have most sympathy with? Explain your answer below.

Unit 6: Dramatic! — Section 5 Crafting characters

Set extension activity

3a Make some notes outlining everything that you are told, or can infer, about the characters of Flora and Max from the extract on page 236 of the Student Book.

Flora: _____

_____

_____

_____

_____

_____

Max: _____

_____

_____

_____

_____

_____

b You have been asked to write background character descriptions for Max and Flora, to help actors understand the characters they are going to play. Use the notes you made in **Activity 3a**, as well as your own imagination, to describe each character. For example, in addition to describing their personalities and appearance, you could add in imagined details such as what they enjoy doing with friends to give a fuller impression of them.

Flora: _____

_____

_____

_____

_____

_____

Max: _____

_____

_____

_____

_____

Referring back using pronouns

4 Rewrite the sentences below, replacing the repeated words with pronouns.

a Max wants Flora to sell part of her garden. Max tries various ways to persuade Flora.

_____

_____

b Flora ignores Max's attempts to persuade her to sell part of her garden. Instead, Flora asks Max to help her with the apples.

_____

_____

c Max and Flora are in conflict. Max and Flora want very different things.

_____

_____

Writing a response to characters

5 You are going to write one paragraph responding to the writer's presentation of Max in the extract. Think about:
- how the way Max speaks reveals his intentions
- how the playwright wants the audience to respond to the character.

a Write one or two sentences that make a key point, stating an impression of Max that the writer intended to create.

_____

_____

_____

_____

b Write another one or two sentences that include a short, focused quotation giving evidence for your point.

_____

_____

_____

c Write one or two more sentences to complete your paragraph, explaining how your evidence proves your point, and how the writer's choices help to achieve their intention.

_____

_____

_____

Unit 6: Dramatic! — Section 5 Crafting characters

Set extension activity

6 Revise the skills you have covered in the first half of this unit, ready for the assessment in the next lesson. You may find it helpful to note down the key points covered in each of the sections so far. If there are any areas where you do not feel confident, reread the appropriate pages in the Student Book.

Section 1: Curtain up

Use the stage directions to infer information about the characters.

Section 2: Setting the scene

Section 3: From page to page

Section 4: Creating conflict

Section 5: Crafting characters

Section 6
Assessment

In this section, you will answer questions on a short extract and improve a sample response from a student.

In this extract, two friends have just won a large amount of money in an art competition they entered together. The rules of the competition state that they must agree together whether to give the money to charity or keep it for themselves.

▼ Read the extract and then answer the questions that follow it.

1 Taj We should give it to charity

    Ali You know we're not going to. Seize the day!

    Taj It's the right thing to do.

    Ali What are you talking about? Imagine what we can do with all this!

5 Taj Someone'll need it more than us.

    Ali (*eyes closed*) A lifetime's supply of sweets.

    Taj School for example. They haven't bought any new books for years.

    Ali A car. Convertible maybe.

    Taj We can't drive!

10 Ali You could get some trainers that fit and don't have holes in. (*pointing at his own shoes*) Like these babies!

    Taj Shut up! It's not my fault I haven't got any money! You've got enough anyway, why d'you want more?

    Ali (*opening his eyes and looking sideways at Taj*) How about your Dad?

    Taj (*bitterly*) What? You think I should blame him?

15 Ali No, stupid. What about your Dad's operation?

    (*Pause*)

    Taj Oh.

    Ali Too expensive you were saying.

    Taj (*hands over his face*) Don't.

20 Ali Not now it isn't. Doesn't have to be anyway. All we have to do is…

    (*Pause, then, very slowly, Taj nods his head*)

Assessment questions

1 Look at the first five lines. What is it that the friends are disagreeing about?

_____

2 Ali suggests four reasons that Taj should want to take the money. What are they?

_____

_____

Unit 6: Dramatic!   **Section 6 Assessment**

3 Which stage direction suggests that Ali is trying to manipulate Taj?

4 What can you infer about how old the characters are? Explain your answer below.

5 What does the extract imply about Taj's family? Write a short paragraph explaining your answer.

6 Look at the following question and read the student's response that follows.

Question: What impression has the writer created of the two characters?

Response: Their two friends who win some money in a competition and their arguing about what to do. Ali wants to buy a sweetshop and a car and Taj thinks they should give it all away. In the end they probably going to take the money because Ali persuades Taj by teasing him about his trainers which have holes in.

Taj seems quite good and Ali seems quite funny selfish and that's why they probably going to take the money.

a What advice would you give to this student to help them improve their response?

b Write your own improved response to the question in the space below. Write at least two paragraphs.

Section 7
Shakespearean speech

In this section, you will practise exploring Shakespeare's language, and how he uses dialogue to develop characters and relationships.

Checking understanding

1 Look again at the *King Lear* extracts on page 242 of the Student Book.

a Which daughter is older? Write down a quotation that gives this information.

b Why does Goneril exaggerate her love so much?

c In the first lines of the second extract, what is King Lear asking Cordelia to do?

Responding to dialogue

2 Based on what you have read and inferred from the extracts, write one or two sentences explaining what you think is the most important thing to:

a Goneril:

b King Lear:

c Cordelia:

3 What does King Lear mean when he says 'Nothing will come of nothing'?

4 Explain what you think will happen to the three characters as the play progresses.

Unit 6: Dramatic! — Section 7 Shakespearean speech

Set extension activity

5 You have been asked to write descriptions of the three characters: King Lear, Goneril and Cordelia. Your descriptions will help actors who are going to play the three roles to understand the characters' personalities, what is important to them, and how they feel about each other. Use your imagination to add to the impression you get from the extracts on page 242 of the Student Book.

King Lear: _____

_____

_____

_____

_____

_____

_____

Goneril: _____

_____

_____

_____

_____

_____

_____

_____

_____

_____

_____

Cordelia: _____

_____

_____

_____

_____

_____

_____

_____

Exploring dialogue

6 How do you imagine each of the characters feels at the end of the extracts? Write one or two sentences for each character based on their dialogue, explaining your answer.

King Lear: _____

_____

_____

Goneril: _____

_____

_____

Cordelia: _____

_____

_____

7 How does King Lear's speech show that his emotions change through the course of the second extract? Explain your answer below.

_____

_____

_____

Planning a script

8 You are going to plan a scene similar to the *King Lear* extract. A student has been told that he or she can invite one of their friends to come on a family holiday with them. The student tells two friends that one of them will be picked, and asks them to explain which one should be picked. One friend is manipulative and dishonest. The other is truthful.

Make some notes describing each of the three characters, including their personalities, how they feel about one another, and what is most important to each of them.

Character 1: _____

_____

_____

Character 2: _____

_____

_____

Character 3: _____

_____

Set extension activity

9a Continue to plan the script that you began to think about in **Activity 8**, using the following prompts.

(i) How will each character speak? What kind of sentences and vocabulary will they use?

_____
_____
_____
_____
_____

(ii) How will the student who has to pick one person react to each of his or her friends?

_____
_____
_____
_____
_____

b Now write your script in the space below, remembering to use dialogue to create an impression of each character. Continue your answer in your notebook if needed.

_____
_____
_____
_____
_____
_____
_____
_____
_____
_____
_____
_____
_____
_____

Section 8
Performing

This section links to pages 246–249 of the Student Book.

In this section, you will practise exploring how performing a scene in different ways can change your response to characters and events.

Understanding the text

1 Read these lines of dialogue from the extract on page 246 of the Student Book and answer the questions that follow.

> Queen   Come, come, you answer with an idle tongue.
>
> Hamlet   Go, go, you question with a wicked tongue.

a Explain what these lines tell us about how Queen Gertrude and Hamlet feel about each other.

_____

_____

b Why is Queen Gertrude annoyed with Hamlet? Explain your answer below.

_____

_____

c Why is Hamlet angry with Queen Gertrude? Explain your answer below.

_____

_____

Shakespeare's language

2 Rewrite the dialogue (but not the stage directions) in the extract from *Hamlet* on page 246 of the Student Book, using modern English but retaining the same meaning. Continue your answer in your notebook.

_____

_____

_____

_____

_____

_____

Unit 6: Dramatic! — Section 8 Performing

Set extension activity

3 For each of the lines below from the extract, write a sentence describing how the line should be spoken. This could include description of tone of voice, facial expression or physical action.

| Hamlet | Now, mother, what's the matter? |

| Queen | Hamlet, thou hast thy father much offended. |

| Hamlet | Mother, you have my father much offended. |

| Queen | Come, come, you answer with an idle tongue. |

| Hamlet | Go, go, you question with a wicked tongue. |

| Queen | Why, how now, Hamlet! |

| Hamlet | What's the matter now? |

| Queen | Have you forgot me? |

| Hamlet | No, by the rood, not so:
 You are the queen, your husband's brother's wife;
 And, — would it were not so! — you are my mother. |

| Queen | Nay, then, I'll set those to you that can speak. |

| Hamlet | Come, come, and sit you down; you shall not budge;
 You go not til I set you up a glass
 Where you may see the inmost part of you. |

| Queen | What wilt thou do? Thou wilt not murder me?
 Help, help, ho! |

Writing a response

4 You are going to plan and write a response to the following task: What impression do you get of the relationship between Hamlet and his mother in the extract on page 246 of the Student Book? Make some notes using the following prompts.

a How does Hamlet feel about his mother at the beginning of the extract? Note down what Hamlet feels and why he feels it, with quotations from the extract.

_____
_____
_____

b How does Queen Gertrude feel about Hamlet at the beginning of the extract? Note down what she feels and why she feels it, with quotations from the extract.

_____
_____
_____

c How do Hamlet's emotions change throughout the extract?

_____
_____

d Why do Hamlet's emotions change?

_____
_____

e Note down one or two quotations that show how Hamlet's emotions change.

_____
_____

f How do Queen Gertrude's emotions change throughout the extract?

_____
_____

g Why do Queen Gertrude's emotions change?

_____
_____

h Note down one or two quotations that show how Queen Gertrude's emotions change.

_____
_____

Set extension activity

5 Continue to plan your response to the task: What impression do you get of the relationship between Hamlet and his mother in the extract on page 246 of the Student Book?

a Note down some ideas about how Shakespeare's language choices create that impression.

_____
_____
_____
_____
_____
_____
_____

b Now write your response to the task in the space below. Write two or three paragraphs. Continue your answer in your notebook if needed. Remember to:
- comment on the relationship and how it changes
- use short quotations to support the points you make
- explain how language choices create an impression of the relationship.

_____
_____
_____
_____
_____
_____
_____
_____
_____
_____
_____
_____
_____
_____

Section 9
Exploring themes

In this section, you will practise exploring the theme of power in Shakespeare's play *Macbeth*.

Understanding

1a Look again at the extract on page 250 of the Student Book. In one paragraph, summarise the conversation between Lady Macbeth and her husband.

_____
_____
_____
_____

b Why do you think Lady Macbeth is so keen to stick to the plan and kill the king? Explain your answer below.

_____
_____
_____
_____

c Based on what you have learned about the characters in the extract, who do you think will win the argument about whether to kill the king? Explain your answer below.

_____
_____
_____
_____

Selecting evidence

2 Write down one quotation from the extract to support each of the following statements.

a Lady Macbeth doubts Macbeth's bravery. _____

b Macbeth begs his wife to stop. _____

c Macbeth is nervous about the risks of the plan. _____

d Lady Macbeth is confident and thinks the risks are worth the reward.

_____

Set extension activity

3 A director who is planning a production of *Macbeth* believes that Lady Macbeth is far more powerful than her husband. She wants to convey this in the way the extract is presented on stage.

a What advice would you give the director? Use the prompts below to structure your ideas.

  (i) What tones of voice should Macbeth and Lady Macbeth use?

  (ii) How should they move around the stage?

  (iii) How should they be dressed?

  (iv) How should they interact with each other?

  (v) What kind of sound and lighting effects would you recommend for this scene?

b Write a paragraph or two explaining how your suggestions will help to convey the sense that Lady Macbeth is more powerful.

Exploring the theme of power

4a In the play, Macbeth plans to kill the king, then thinks better of it. What does this suggest about his attitude to power? Write a sentence or two explaining your answer below.

_____
_____
_____

b Lady Macbeth is determined to persuade her husband to kill the king. What does this suggest about her attitude to power? Write a sentence or two explaining your answer below.

_____
_____
_____

c How does Lady Macbeth try to bully Macbeth into killing the king? Write a paragraph explaining your answer below, using quotations from the extract on page 250 of the Student Book.

_____
_____
_____
_____
_____

d How does Macbeth try to resist Lady Macbeth's power? Write a paragraph explaining your answer below, using quotations from the extract to support the points you make.

_____
_____
_____
_____
_____

Reviewing sentence structure

5 Look at your answers to **Activities 4c and 4d**. Are your key points clear? Could you make them any clearer by changing your choice of sentence structure? Rewrite one of your answers below. Ensure that you make a clear point, support it with the most relevant quotation and explain how the quotation links to your point.

_____
_____
_____
_____
_____

Set extension activity

6 You are going to plan and write a response to this task: What impression do you get of the relationship between Macbeth and Lady Macbeth in the extract on page 250 of the Student Book?

a Look back over what you have written in the previous three pages of this Workbook and note down the key points and evidence that you will include in your answer.

b Now write your response in the space below. Continue your answer in your notebook if needed.

Section 10
Introductions and conclusions

In this section, you will practise developing your critical writing skills, exploring ways of introducing and concluding your responses.

Understanding

1a What gives Lady Macbeth the impression that Macbeth is losing his mind? Explain your answer below, using relevant evidence from the extract on page 254 of the Student Book.

_____
_____
_____

b How does Lady Macbeth criticise or mock her husband in her final speech in this extract? Explain your answer below.

_____
_____
_____

Planning a response

2 You are going to plan a response to the following question: What impression does Lady Macbeth's reaction to Macbeth in this extract create of her character?
Note down any ideas you have, along with relevant quotations to support them.

a What does Lady Macbeth think of her husband? What impression does this create of her?

_____
_____
_____

b How does she try to persuade him to act? What impression does this create of her?

_____
_____
_____

c What does she plan to do herself? What impression does this create of her?

_____
_____
_____

Unit 6: Dramatic! Section 10 Introductions and conclusions

Set extension activity

3a Using the ideas you wrote down in **Activity 2**, write three paragraphs in response to the following question: What impression does Lady Macbeth's reaction to Macbeth in this extract create of her character?

In each paragraph, make sure you make a clear point, back it up with relevant evidence, and explain how the evidence links to the point. Continue your answer in your notebook if needed.

b Look back over your writing and correct any errors in spelling, punctuation and grammar.

c Identify any opportunities to improve the vocabulary you have used, and make the relevant changes to your response.

Introductions

4 Write a one-sentence or two-sentence introduction to the response you wrote for **Activity 3a**. You could begin: *In this extract, Lady Macbeth reacts...*

Proofreading

5a There are four words missing from this paragraph. Mark where the words are missing with a pen.

> Macbeth is weak character. He seems to be losing his mind after killing the king, which he only did because his wife told to. Lady Macbeth tries persuade him to snap out of it but he cannot and she announces she take the daggers herself.

b Now rewrite the paragraph, correcting all the errors you found.

6 There are some comma splice errors in the following paragraph. Rewrite the paragraph, replacing the incorrect commas with either full stops and capital letters, or conjunctions.

> When she realises that Macbeth is losing his mind, Lady Macbeth is worried, she tries to talk him to his senses, he is too shaken to go back with the daggers, she decides to do it for him.

Conclusions

7a Look back through what you wrote in your response for **Activity 3a** on the previous page. In one or two sentences, summarise the points you have made in each of the three paragraphs.

b Finish your conclusion by writing one or two sentences to comment on the impact Shakespeare intended Lady Macbeth's reaction to Macbeth to have on the audience.

Set extension activity

8 Revise the skills you have covered in the second half of this unit, ready for the assessment in the next lesson. You may find it helpful to note down the key points covered in each of the sections so far. If there are any areas where you do not feel confident, reread the appropriate pages in the Student Book. Think back to when you planned for the previous assessment. What helped? What could you improve on?

Section 7: Shakespearean speech

Check your understanding of a text by answering questions about it.

Section 8: Performing

Section 9: Exploring themes

Section 10: Introductions and conclusions

Section 11
Assessment

In this section, you will identify the mistakes in a sample response from a student and write an improved version.

In this extract from William Shakespeare's *Macbeth*, Macbeth has killed the king, become king himself, and murdered his former ally Banquo, whom he saw as a threat. Sitting at dinner with several other characters, Macbeth has just seen the ghost of Banquo at the end of the table, pointing at him. Nobody else can see the ghost.

▼ Read the extract and then answer the questions that follow it.

1	Ross	Gentlemen, rise: his highness is not well.
	Lady Macbeth	Sit, worthy friends: my lord is often thus,
		And hath been from his youth: pray you, keep seat;
		The fit is momentary; upon a thought
5		He will again be well: if much you note him,
		You shall offend him and extend his passion:
		Feed, and regard him not. Are you a man?
	Macbeth	Ay, and a bold one, that dare look on that
		Which might appal the devil.
10	Lady Macbeth	O proper stuff!
		This is the very painting of your fear:
		This is the air-drawn dagger which, you said,
		Led you to Duncan. O, these flaws and starts,
		Impostors to true fear, would well become
15		A woman's story at a winter's fire,
		Authorized by her grandam. Shame itself!
		Why do you make such faces? When all's done,
		You look but on a stool.

1 Look at the following question and read the student's response that follows.

Question: What impression does Shakespeare create of Lady Macbeth in this extract?

Response: Lady Macbeth is trying to tell everyone not to pay much attention to Macbeths strange behavier. Then she is quite anoyed and tells his he is not a man and that hes making things up and he isn't really scared of them because its like a silly story told by a grandmother. She said he should be ashamed and to stop making a fuss and that all he could see is a stool so she doesnt believe him. But Macbeth is really scarred because he has seen the ghost.

Unit 6: Dramatic!   Section 11 Assessment   245

You are going to improve and extend this response.

   a Underline any spelling or punctuation mistakes.
   b Underline any verbs that are in the wrong tense.
   c Write a 'V' next to any opportunities to improve the impact of the writing by making different vocabulary choices.
   d Write an 'S' next to any opportunities to improve the impact of the writing by varying sentence length and structure.
   e Use the space in the box below to make some notes and plan how you will improve and extend this answer.

2 Rewrite your improved version of the answer in the space below. Continue your answer in your notebook. Remember to:
- use quotations
- describe the impression created
- comment on how the writer created that impression
- write at least three paragraphs.

Notes

Notes

Published by Pearson Education Limited, 80 Strand, London, WC2R 0RL.
www.pearsonglobalschools.com

Text © Pearson Education Limited 2020
Designed by Pearson Education Limited 2020
Typeset by PDQ Digital Media Solutions Ltd
Project managed by Just Content Ltd
Produced by Just Content Ltd and Danielle Whisker
Edited by Judith John, Liliane Nénot and Judith Shaw
Cover design © Pearson Education Limited 2020
With thanks to Carole Sunderland
Illustrated by Beehive Illustration
Cover design © Pearson Education Limited 2020

Cover images: Busakorn Pongparnit/Getty Images

The right of Ben Hulme-Cross to be identified as authors of this work has been asserted by him in accordance with the Copyright, Designs and Patents Act 1988.

First published 2020

27 26 25
10 9 8

British Library Cataloguing in Publication Data
A catalogue record for this book is available from the British Library

ISBN 978 0 435 20079 4

Copyright notice
All rights reserved. No part of this publication may be reproduced in any form or by any means (including photocopying or storing it in any medium by electronic means and whether or not transiently or incidentally to some other use of this publication) without the written permission of the copyright owner, except in accordance with the provisions of the Copyright, Designs and Patents Act 1988 or under the terms of a licence issued by the Copyright Licensing Agency, 5th Floor, Shackleton House, 4 Battlebridge Lane, London, SE1 2HX (www.cla.co.uk). Applications for the copyright owner's written permission should be addressed to the publisher.

Printed in Slovakia by Neografia

Acknowledgements

p48: **Comic Company**: Poster of "Water - Everybody's Favourite Drink poster". Used with Permission.